Heaven's Short List!

The Miracles of Jesus, The Son of God!

Sam Thomas
MDiv DDS PhD

Dear Dr Martin

God bless –

Sam Thomas

xulon PRESS

DEDICATED

TO MY WIFE

Hannah

Who taught me how to pray!

Could it be that Grace marches uninvited into the soli-tude of our lives, confronts us when we are at our lowest, explodes into the eclipse of our dark and doomed present, boldly restores us, and drops us speechless at the feet of Jesus?

Preface

As I travel with Jesus through sleepy little villages tucked away in the hills of Galilee, I am reminded time and time again of the way He dealt with people. Heaven had an appointment with the hungry, the sick and the lost! They were on Heaven's shortlist!

When they were hungry, He fed them.
When they were sick, He healed them.
When they were troubled, He comforted them.
When they were lost, He led them home.
When they were in tears He cried with them.
When they were held in Satan's grasp, He freed them.

What kind of a Man was He? Can I be like Him? Can I touch the untouchable? Can I touch a leper with my hands? Do I stop just long enough along life's busy pathways and bring relief to those that are hurting? This Man who went about healing amazes me!

What was God like? What was the first face that the blind men saw when they were healed? What was the first voice that the deaf heard? What were the first words that the dumb spoke when He healed them?

I am touched and moved by this Man, Jesus, *ben-Yosef* (The Son of Joseph). He could command the storms in the sea to cease. At the same time He would weep over the tomb of His friend Lazarus.

He worried about the insufficient amount of wine that was present at a busy wedding at Cana. Yet as He was being led away to be executed, He would stop just long enough to attach the ear of the High Priest's servant. Everyone mattered to Him.
They all belonged to Him.

Walk with Him as you read these pages. See how He touched the untouchable. Ask Him to touch you.
You will never be the same again!

Who Is This Jesus?

In Genesis He is the Sacrifice for your souls.
In Exodus He is the Blood on the doorposts.
In Leviticus He is the Shekinah Glory.
In Numbers He is the Bronze Serpent.
In Deuteronomy He is the City of Refuge.

In Joshua He is the Warrior God.
In Judges He is the Sustainer of Laws.
In Ruth He is the Redeemer of the Forgotten.
In Samuel 1 and 2 He is the Rock of Israel.

In Kings 1 and 2 He is the King of Peace.
In Chronicles 1 and 2 He is the Gatekeeper.
In Ezra He is the Transcriber of Laws.

In Nehemiah He is the Wall of Stone around you.
In Esther He is the Silent Voice.
In Job He is the Challenging God.
In Psalms He is your Refuge.
In Proverbs He is the Beginning of Wisdom.

In Ecclesiastes He is the Voice of Reason.
In Song of Solomon He is the Beloved.
In Isaiah He is the Offering for all our Sins.

In Jeremiah He is the Branch.
In Ezekiel He is the Breath that gives life to the dead bones.

In Daniel He is the Coming Messiah, The Prince of Peace.
In Hosea, He is the Relentless Lover.
In Joel He is the Holy Spirit.
In Amos He is the Plumb Line.
In Obadiah He is the Sovereign Lord.

In Jonah He is the One who Forgives.
In Micah He is the Merciful One!
In Nahum He is the Avenging God.
In Habakkuk He is the One from Everlasting.
In Zephaniah He is the Searcher with Lamps!

In Haggai He is the One who chooses you.
In Zechariah He is the Priest and King.
In Malachi He is the One who demands your tithe.

In Mathew He is the King of the Jews.
In Mark He is the Servant.
In Luke He is Son of Man.
In John He is the Word in Flesh.
In Acts He is the Force behind the Early Church.
In Romans He is *"Abba, Father!"*
In Corinthians 1 and 2 He is the Love that never fails.
In Galatians He is the One who gave Himself for me.
In Ephesians He is the Guarantee of our Inheritance.

In Philippians He is the Name above All Names.
In Colossians He is the Image of the Invisible God.
In Thessalonians He is the Resurrection.
In Timothy He is the Savior of Sinners.

In Titus He is the Salvation to all people.
In Philemon He is the Great Emancipator.

In Hebrews He is the High Priest in the Heavenly Sanctuary.
In Peter He is the One who calls you to be holy.

In John1, 2, and 3 He is Love Incarnate.
In Jude He is the One who keeps you from stumbling.
In Revelation He is the Alpha, the Omega, the Beginning and the End and the Glorious Returning King.

Table of Contents

1
The Leper

λεπρος

A man with leprosy came and knelt before him and said,
"Lord, if you are willing, you can make me clean."
Matt 8:2 (NIV)

I was unclean. It was a Divine Punishment! I was a wasted human being living on borrowed time. I was a dead man walking.

The *Torah* clearly stated that if you had leprosy, you were an outcast. Once you were found with leprosy, your house was destroyed—burned to the ground—along with all your earthly possessions and you became an outcast, a man the society did not want! You were cursed by your family, exiled by the priests, and forsaken by *Elohim!* You roamed the hills and lived in caves until that day when death visited you, not too soon! I belonged to the special class of people punished by *Elohim!* I was in the company of *Cain, Miriam, Goliath, Samson, Pharaoh, Uzzah, Naaman, Korah, Dathan and Abiram*, and the list is quite impressive!

Why Lord? Why have You visited me with this curse? Small white patches appeared around my arms, and they spread and became raw, and the raw flesh turned to scabs with no feelings! It was fright-ening! There was nothing I could do! I tried at first to ignore

19

> *I was unclean. It was a Divine Punishment! I was a wasted human being living on borrowed time. I was a dead man walking.*

it, and then it spread to my fingers, toes, nose, face, and chest! I was terrified! I went to the Priests. The pronouncement by the priest that I had the dreaded disease was the nail in the coffin, and it cost me my family and my life. Everyone left me! My wife, my children, my neighbors, and my relatives all fled in terror as this disease invaded me! When you are seen as someone punished by the Divine Elohim, no one wants to be by your side!

Adonai, do You not care? Do You not keep Your own promises of forgiveness and grace and mercy? Just look at me! Is this deformed body filled with pus and scaly skin with lost nerve endings and oozing flesh housed in a contorted cage of skin—*Is this Your Image?* Is this what You intended for me when You knit me together in the secret places of my mother's womb?

"Before I formed you, I knew you!" Rubbish!

"I wove you and knit you in the secret place while you were being formed." Garbage!

Obviously, Lord You did not take too much time to knit!

How ridiculous! I am just an Image of God rotting away in the Galilean wilderness, forever wandering the hills and the empty mountains crying, *"Unclean! Unclean!"* I am waiting for death while my body wastes away and is slowly consumed in the evening by rats chewing on my toes and fingers and a face that felt no pain. It was almost comical! The Image of God was rat food! *Ha!* Anger and resentment well up inside me!

Who cares! No one does! Image of God, cursed by the *Elohim!*

God, are You *really* there? Do You *really* care? Do You even know I exist? There had been no prophet that could cleanse a leper! There could be no God!

The last one who was healed of leprosy was that heathen captain Naaman by prophet Elisha! But even that was considered folklore. I wasn't there! It could have all been a concocted fantasy that was passed from generation to generation with that oral tradition!

And...and this cleansing ritual by the high priests in the temple! *Are You joking?* These priests wouldn't even touch their own wives when their wives had their monthly menstrual cycle! They are supposed to examine a leper? *What a joke!* These pompous keepers of the law had insulated themselves with thousands of laws so that they could never be "unclean!" In fact, these Law keepers, who were supposed to be the mouthpiece of YHWH, were constantly scheming to cheat the society!

Did you really think they had the time to see if I was *clean? Of* course not! Here in this body of bones and punctured skin I shall spend the rest of my days waiting for scraps of food, at the mercy of strangers. . .*Unclean! Unclean! Unclean! Worse than a dog! At least a dog could pick up some scarps of food in a crowded room! I would be stoned if I approached anyone within ten feet!*

What is this commotion I hear? No! What? It can't be!

The blind receive their sight? The lame are walking! The sick are made well!

The maimed are made whole! Demons are sent packing! Whoa!

Wait a minute! Wait a lousy minute! Could this be ELISHA? It's worth a try!

But how do I get past this multitude of people?

How can I get to the front of the crowd? I have to see this *"Prophet. . .this Healer. . .this Person!"*

Maybe! Just maybe if I tried a little harder!

"Go Away! You unclean filthy sinner! Get lost! You leper! Whew! Move away from this man filled with rotten and oozing flesh! Get away, you scum of the earth!"

I see anger in their faces! I see stones gathered to stone me! I see their faces contorted with hatred! *"Stone this man! He is unclean! He is a leper! A leper! A leper! Unclean! Unclean! Move away!"* I see fear mixed with anger and hatred on their faces as I slowly but surely wrap my torn dirty filthy garment around my filthy body. I am prepared for that first rock to hit me! I'd rather die here right now than wander the hills of Galilee for an eternity. . . Life has been hard; I am done with this curse of the gods! Someone please throw that first rock!

O God! O Jehovah! YHWH Shalom! Where are You?

Haven't I suffered enough! Where are You, God?

Where is this Miracle Worker? Just maybe. . .just maybe He can find me!

Then it happened. It was as though I was being guided by a Divine Hand that propelled me forward forcefully to the presence of One greater than this disease that had held me in its clutches all these years! *He was there!* There was something about this Man! I was desperate! He was waiting! I was troubled! He was at peace!

I fell at His feet! *"Lord, Adonai, Master, Prophet, Can you heal a filthy unclean leper who has nothing? I beg You! Is it possible? Can You? These years of pain and misery have been hard on me! I am a walking dead man! Help me! Please!"*

Tears of anger and pain burst from my bleary red and motionless eyes that had long ago forgotten how to blink and surprised the swarm of flies feasting on my sores that were festering my cheeks!

He spoke! *"I have been waiting for You! I have been longing to heal you! I will heal you! I will touch you! I will take upon me all your sickness and pain and suffering! I will be your walking dead! Yes! Be made well!"*

What! Is He serious? He will *touch* me? Does He know that He would need a ritual cleaning? Is He serious?

With that He touched me and made me whole! Just like that. . .One moment a leper and the next moment I was clean, whole, and healthy. . .Just like that! *Instantaneous!* I did not have to dip myself into the Jordan River like Naaman had to or wash myself in a pool in Jerusalem! None of that! I was made whole by the touch of this Man Jesus! He touched me and made me whole!

It is a simple story, but it is my personal perfect story! I was a leper. But that day Jesus touched me and made me whole, no longer a leper but a Child of YHWH! In the image of YHWH, perfect!

Let me leave you with this one thought: It doesn't matter who you are, a priest or a leper! You are a walking dead man until Jesus touches you; you are a leper, just like me! I lived in the caves of Galilee. I was rejected, forlorn, and without hope. No one wanted me. They all forsook me and fled at my approach. I thought that I was the one who was punished by Jehovah, but I was the one who was touched by the Son of the Most High God. Only God could curse me, and only God could remove this curse! Thank God, I am restored to myself, my family and to my God!

Hallelujah, thank you, Jesus!

2
Rome's Centurion

εκατονταρχος

When Jesus had entered Capernaum, a centurion came to
him, asking for help. "Lord," he said, "my servant lies at
home paralyzed, suffering terribly."
Matt 8:5,6 (NIV)

One hundred soldiers armed with shields, swords, and body
armor, led by a centurion on a black horse, marched down the
city street! They instilled the terror of Zeus into the provincial hearts
of the peasants of Judea! And Galilee was no exception! Respect the
Romans or else suffer severe punishment! Disobedience to the laws
of Rome had grave consequences!

*I was the backbone of the Roman army. We were the legionnaires
that guarded and protected the interest of Caesar and the Roman
Senate. Our allegiance was to the Roman Eagle!*

It has been a long time since I went back home! Rome was
beautiful! Rome haunted my memories and many a sleepless night I
had drifted off dreaming about the wonder of Rome: the gladiators,
the Arena, the Forum, the Apian Way, The Old City, the chariot
races, fine wine, the warm Roman baths and the gentle yet peaceful
countryside. Soft women with olive-colored skin who smelled of

23

I was the backbone of the Roman army. We were the legionnaires that guarded and protected the interest of Caesar and the Roman Senate. Our allegiance was to the Roman Eagle!

perfumes from Capri possessed my mind! It was nothing like this desolate patch of dry hills that commanded my constant vigilance! *Ah! I am so disgusted!*

When they told me I was to lead a garrison of Roman soldiers into Judea, I was excited. It was my first command outside Rome! I would be the *Peacekeeper.* The city of Tiberius was only an hour away on horseback from Capernaum and Ptolemais' Seaport only 20 miles away. How bad can it be? And *"Pax Romana"* had been set in motion by Emperor Augustus, and there were no wars to fight.

This shouldn't be too bad! In fact I had heard that Capernaum was a jewel on the coast of the sea of Tiberius.

Little did I know!

But here I was, stationed in the Roman garrison of Capernaum, the rough and tough fishing village that was tucked away in the northern-most shores of the blue shimmering shores of Lake Tiberius. You think the Roman soldiers are bad! I've got news for you! These foul mouthed, hard-core, no-nonsense Galilean fishermen, who would stab you in broad daylight for the price of a few pickled sardines, were the toughest I have ever encountered.

So Rome had to keep order since Capernaum was full of these dirty hard-drinking fishermen. We needed their tax and fish and they in turn needed to be controlled! I was to enforce their salt tax, fish tax, fruit tax, grain tax, and produce tax! I was the Roman centurion who would keep peace in this fishing village and make sure that Caesar received his full tax and all violence was quenched. The buck stopped with me, unlike Jerusalem, where the Jews had their temple, their temple guards, and the corrupt system of peace keeping and compromised courts!

They said I would be in Capernaum just for a few days, and then, I would be back in my beloved Rome. Two weeks at the most. . .Little did I know. . .*Boring! Difficult!* You could say I was wasting away. I was just a Roman centurion trying to police the local fisherman. Instead of fighting wars in some distant Roman province, under the Roman Eagle, here I was trapped in a smelly, dirty, fishermen's village. What a waste. *Rome had tricked me!* Caesar should never have sent me to this despicable, dirty hole-in-the-wall village!

So like all soldiers, I had selected a few of the local boys in town to be my servants. I grew fond of this one Judean lad. He was not more than 14 years of age. He was my personal servant. You know, the one that comes running to you when you enter your quarters and unties your shoes and the body armor and brings you a jug of water to wash your face and has the cup of sweet wine in his hand to quench your thirst. There was something about this kid. He was always there. He was an orphan, and I was his family. Day after day and month after month he was in my service faithfully washing my feet, polishing my sword and tying my shoes. He made life tolerable. He was indispensable. A small little light of innocence and loyalty had wormed itself into this tough and hard and unforgiving heart of mine, one who despised every minute in Capernaum!

One day I came home from my duties, and the boy wasn't there. He had been replaced! I was furious! I called the steward in charge that fake tub of fatness that pretended he was the purser to Caesar himself!

"Where is the lad?" I thundered. *"Who relieved him of his duties?"* I had learned to trust this boy! I knew that my life was in danger every time I turned my back to some stranger! This boy had been in my service, and I needed him!

"Where is he, you tub of fat? Bring him to me! NOW!"

"O most gracious Caesar, the boy is sick. He is dying!" The tub of fatness squeaked, wringing his hands.

"WHAT! How can this be? Did you poison him? Did you whip him? Did you punish him? I want to see him!"

So off I went to look for this lad and found him in his small and dark quarters. My own personal physician was treating him. There he stood with some concoction in his hand that only the gods knew, and he sadly shook his head as his eyes met mine!

The boy was shivering! His pale forehead was hot! His eyes so full of innocence were tormented with pain! The corners of his mouth writhed in some unknown agony! I could not bear to look! How could this be? He was fine this morning! Did that tub of fatness poison him? I would have him skewered and roasted in slow flames for having caused this sickness! I reached out to the boy!

The tub of fatness spoke! *"O great Cesar, do not touch the boy! He will be dead within the hour. You might catch this unknown disease, and there is no one to cure him now! He will be dead soon enough!"*

I rushed out into the Galilean night! Wasn't there something that could be done? This slave boy who had become like my own son! I had heard about this miracle worker that roamed the Judean hills. He was a Nazarene. We Romans believed that the sons of the gods visited the earth now and then, healing and setting things right! Maybe, just maybe if I found this healer; maybe he is one of Zeus's offspring! Maybe he could heal this lad who had been so faithful to me. I had heard whispers of blind men receiving their eyesight, lepers being cleansed, thousands being fed, and storms being calmed! Tales! Tales! Stories! But I had no proof! I would seek this man—or was he a god! Who knows! All I wanted was the lad to be made well!

I mounted my horse and, accompanied by Atilius, my soldier in command, sped out into the foggy Galilean night. My quest for the gods had begun!

"Have you seen the miracle worker?" Atilius asked a drunken fisherman.

"Get away you Roman Dog!" the drunken voice answered back!

In frustration we searched what seemed like hours, from one wine house to another, from one fishing boat to another. I was tired. The night had taken its course. Soon it would be morning, and I would have to get ready for a funeral. I just could not shake the dying look of that innocent lad! But maybe it was not meant to be! Death is a sweet welcome to those that waste in pain!

And then I noticed a group of people gathered around in the early morning hours listening to a man seated on the beach! It might be my last chance; maybe they might know where this Nazarene was! Atilius and I dismounted and made our way to the edge of the crowd!

"Roman Dog! Filthy Gentile!" Words of hatred and looks that could kill Augustus himself lashed at us.

"You here," Atilius *shouted. " have you seen the miracle worker. The centurion desires a word with him!"*

"Sir," a lady with a basket replied, "He is here!"

WHAT! I could barely believe my ears. The Miracle worker, the son of Zeus, the incarnation of the gods is HERE? I could not wait. I made way through the crowds to the front of the crowd!

I saw him there!

Years of emotion that had welled up in my heart burst forth! *"Son of the holy gods. Could you heal my lad, my servant boy who is dying?"*

He answered. *"I will. Take me to him!"*

Did I hear that right? The incarnation of Zeus himself wants to visit my garrison. There was no way that this could happen.

"Just a command, Lord. . . . Just a word. . Just a whisper. . Just a glance. . .That is all I need from you. You do not need to come!"

I could not believe I was conversing with the gods!

He spoke. *"According to your faith may it be done. Go! Your servant is made well!"*

That is all I needed. I knew the gods have spoken. As I left I heard something about faith; I don't recall anything much.

Atilius and I sped home, and as we neared the garrison, there stood the tub of fatness and my precious little lad.

The boy would serve me for years. . . .

A few years later I heard that the miracle worker was impaled to a tree and died in Jerusalem. I also heard around the campfires that the Roman soldiers who stood watch at that tomb witnessed his resurrection.

Tales! Stories around a Roman campfire? I wish I knew!

All I know is that my servant was healed by the gods!

I wish I had some profound words to tell you. But I will tell you this as a Roman Centurion in the army of Augustus, Emperor of Rome, this man was a god. If the stories are true, if the stories that say that the Miracle Worker was in fact raised from the dead, and if these stories are true, find him like I did, and he will talk to you. He might even want to visit you. He talked to me, a Roman Centurion who hated Galilee and the dirty filthy town of Capernaum..

You are not any worse off than I was!

3

The Mother-in-Law

πενθεραν

When Jesus came into Peter's house,
he saw Peter's mother-in-law lying in bed with a fever.
Matt 8:14 (NIV)

B oy can she cook fish!
Her recipe was the best. Even better than my wife's! I longed to bring home some musht fish from Lake Tiberius and watch her cook that fish. She would clean the fish, remove the scales, and ever so gently rub some spices on the flesh while she mixed

3 tablespoons of strong vinegar and added
2 tablespoons garum, with ground fish paste along with
9 tablespoons olive oil and 4 finely chopped shallots,
1 teaspoon pepper, 1 teaspoon lovage seeds, and a handful of chopped mint.

She would put all the vinaigrette ingredients into a jar and shake it well to blend them together.

She would then brush the musht fillets tenderly with oil, pepper, and salt. She would grill them on one side over the hot coals with that concoction of paste inside the belly of the fish!

She would then turn them and brush the roasted side with the vinaigrette. She even talked to the fish as she cooked!

She was careful not to over-cook, and the flesh should be pink inside.

And the aroma would fill the Galilean hillside.

Boy! Could she cook! Nothing was left to chance.

She was a perfectionist in her kitchen!

It seemed all heaven stopped to listen to my simple request, a healing for someone that meant a lot to me. Is this what is meant by intercessory prayer? I had so much growing to do!

The other thing that she did was take care of strangers! Whenever someone came from out of town, they came to the fisherman's house, courtesy of my mother-in-law. It seemed like she attracted them. She would find total strangers in the market place and bring them home! She would cite the stories of Abraham and the angels he entertained and would insist in her own Galilean drawl,

"The only reason Lot wasn't burned up was because he was a good Jew who sat at the gates of Sodom waiting for strangers!"

I would argue that none, not a single one, of these "angelic strangers" she brought to our house looked anything or resembled in any way, shape, or form "angels" from heaven. They looked more like. . . .well, I won't indulge!

And the arguments over what that neighbor said to this one and why she is marrying that one and why the children are so bad these days and why the Messiah would never come and what happened today at the well would lull me to sleep! She had a sweet but strong voice that hovered over the evening sky!

And her *tefillas!* Ah! I am sure heaven stopped to listen to those fervent prayers from the lips of this pleading woman who would close each sunset with a *tefilla* and greet every sun rise with a *Hillel* to the Creator!

Ah! She was the best! She was an integral part of my family and an indispensable member of Capernaum. There is a saying that behind every good fisherman is a strong woman; this was she!

Today, as I entered the house, I noticed that the house was quiet! *"Wife! Why is the house so quiet? Where is everyone?"* I bellowed!

"Shhhhh! Simon! She is burning up with fever!" My wife replied. *"She has been sick all day. Rabbi Eretz even visited us today, and he can't find out what is wrong with her. She has the chills and has not eaten!"*

"Ah! Woman!" I replied. *"Your mother was bred in the Judean hillside and grew up on the shores of this great sea! Nothing can keep her down! She'll be up in the morning! Now stop fussing over her and bring me some of that turnip soup, some dried sardines, and some bread!"*

Her health declined, slowly but steadily. Our house lost its luster. I hated coming home. I missed her jokes, her cooking, her look, her concern, her boisterous voice that could rattle the bones of a tough fisherman! Yet she was hanging on—barely.

Rabbi Eretz visited us many times with the hope of performing a funeral. I dare say that he was disappointed!

Then it dawned on me!

Hold on! Couldn't the Master heal my mother-in-law? Would he? He had healed total strangers. He had cast out demons, given sight to the blind, and made the lame walk, but they were all strangers. He had not stepped into our personal realm, not yet, anyway! It's worth a try! Should I? What would the other eleven say? What if he said, *"No!"* Would I still follow him if he refused? Would He refuse? We have left everything to follow him; can I ask him? Should I? What would others say?

I fought with questions all night long.

In the morning I knew she was dying. It was the Shabbat! Would the Master even "work" on the Shabbat? Maybe if I asked Him today, He would come to the house tomorrow or the next day and heal her, just maybe! He was so busy all the time, and I hated to impose on Him! I had no choice! I had no options. This was it! I would approach the Master and ask him. Quietly I would ask him so that even if he refused, it would only be between me and Him! I would give Him a way out!

"Master! I know today is the Shabbat! But I have a small request. My mother-in-law is sick! Can you heal her? Maybe after the Shabbat is over, a small visit to my house and a prayer, just a word and she will be made well! She is special to me! She is a wonderful. . . ." I whispered. I did not want the others to know!

He cut me short in the middle of my request.

"Simon! I know all about her! I have been waiting for you to ask me! Have you been with me so long that you forgot that anything that affects you in the tiniest way, affects me? Come on, let's go to your house!"

I could not believe this! *Now?* On the Shabbat? What would the Rabbis say? It is one thing to heal a blind man on the Shabbat, but to heal the mother-in-law of your disciple on the holy Shabbat?

He would come to my house and heal my mother-in-law on the holy Shabbat! Can you imagine the crowd and hushed whispers that followed the Master to my house?

It seemed all heaven stopped to listen to my simple request, a healing for someone that meant a lot to me. Is this what is meant by intercessory prayer? I had so much growing to do!

God entered my house that Shabbat day and touched the one person that had brought so much happiness to my family! She was instantly healed when he touched her!

Heaven entered my house and restored dying earth! She received the true Shabbat blessing! *Baruch atah Adonai mikadesh ha-Shabbat.* (Praised are You, LORD, for the Sabbath and its holiness.)

What can I say? That was the most wonderful *Shabbat* blessing I received!

Nobody, nothing is insignificant to the Master. I have learned over the years that all I have to do is ask Him and He will answer me. Incidentally, my mother-in-law is still going strong, and her arguments are making sense, and her cooking has improved!

Signed
The Fisherman!

31

(Note: Jesus would perform seven very poignant miracles on the Shabbat! And this would infuriate the rabbis so much so that they plotted to get rid of Him. How sad!

He would heal a lame man by the pool of Bethesda John 5:1–18;
He would drive out an evil spirit Mark 1:21–28;
He would heal Peter's mother-in-law Mark 1:29–31;
He would heal a man with a withered hand Luke 6:6;
He would heal a blind man John 9:1–16;
A crippled woman would walk again! Luke 13:10–17;
A man with dropsy would live to see another day! Luke 14:1–6)

****

4
The Storm

σεισμος

*Suddenly a furious storm came up on the lake,
so that the waves swept over the boat.
Matt 8:24 (NIV)*

*V*ia Maris! The *"Way of the Sea"* connected the Egyptian empire to Mesopotamia and passed through the Sea of Galilee. It was a major trade route! If you followed the watering holes, you could safely travel from Memphis in Egypt to Aqaba in the Sinai to Petra in Jordan to the Sea of Galilee in Judea to Damascus and Haran in Syria to Sippur and finally reach Babylon in Mesopotamia! All you had to do was connect the *King's Highway* to *Via Maris!*

My story begins in the Sea of Galilee on the *Via Maris* trade route. I need to tell you a little about this *"Sea."* The Romans called it the *Sea of Tiberius* (after the Roman emperor Tiberius, a name given by the sly King Herod). The Zealot called it the *Sea of Chinneroth,* because they claimed that the sea was shaped like a lyre. How they figured that is beyond me!

We, the fishermen who fished on this sea called it. . .you guessed, the *Sea of Galilee!* How original! It is approximately 13 miles long, 8 miles wide, and about 150 feet deep!

> *The earth seemed to shake! The winds howled their draconian laughter! The waves struck with merciless precision. We were caught in a perfect storm.*

We loved this sea! The water was warm, and the fishing was great. The only problem was that the sea was unpredictable! You see, high cliffs surrounded this sea, and the warm air from the hills and the cold wet air from this sea collided and brought about some spectacular storms without any warning! Instant frightening hurricanes! And these storms were deadly! We had lost many boats and hundreds of fishermen in these waters. The Romans claimed that *Neptune,* the god of the sea, and *Ceres,* the god of the earth, staged their wars right above the Sea of Galilee! These were spectacular shows of force. Howling winds and crashing waves and bolts of lightning and peals of thunder could melt the very heart of a seasoned fisherman!

You took your chances on this sea. But the payout was good. You supplied the travelers on *Via Maris* with fish, and you charged them a pretty *denarius.* We might look rough and daring, but we were businessmen who were wealthy and yes, we paid the taxes and hated the Romans!

So, today was a hard day; we had followed the Master and heard his teachings, and we were ready for a quiet evening on our boats! Did I tell you how beautiful the sea can be when it is quiet? The waves were mesmerizing as they lulled you to sleep. The lap-lap sound of the water on the stern of the boat and the cool evening wet breeze can be a tranquilizer for realities! You forget everything. . .you lose track of time. . .you are relaxed, just numb to the surroundings. Even the Master was asleep tonight! But not us! We were so filled with the events of the day that we started arguing and talking and gesturing and posturing. . .Obviously you are not a Galilean fisherman. You see, when we argue, there is no room for forgiveness, and no one gives in! Time is lost, and words become daggers as we slash each other's throats! And our argument was not about fish and the Romans! It was about who would be the best in the kingdom that the Master would be setting up. Self can swallow itself in the heat of a discussion!

No one realized the storm that was about to destroy us! Who is right and who is wrong was more important than the gale force winds that were about to engulf us. A fraction of a second of self-indulgence and self-glorification, and you lose sight of who is *really in the boat! And what was He doing? Sleeping!*

The earth seemed to shake! The winds howled their draconian laughter! The waves struck with merciless precision. We were caught in a perfect storm. It seemed that the angels of hell were bent upon destroying this tiny little boat. Up we went on a thirty-foot wave and down we came crashing! A few more of these, and the boat would be destroyed! Never in my years of fishing have I come across such a ferocious demonic storm. Was it the wind or was it the demons of hell laughing at us? The thunder roared, and lightening flashed! It seemed that *Zeus* was waging his last battle with *Ceres* and *Neptune!* We were sure that this boat would break into a thousand pieces and we would drown any minute and join the hundreds of boats that lay at the bottom of this deceiving sea!

And then the evening sky was lit by the brightest lightening I had ever seen!

Then I saw him!

He was *sleeping!* WHAT! How could He do that?

How can this man be a sleep? Doesn't he care that we would be killed? Dead? Drowned?

I was reminded of the story that Rabbi Eretz told us about prophet Yonas when he ran away on a boat to *Tarshish* instead of going to *Nineveh.* He had disobeyed God, and God had sent a mighty storm, and the storm ceased when the sailors threw Yonas into the waves! Of course God did provide a giant fish that swallowed him and. . .

But hold on, now that is a thought! Why don't we throw this sleeping man over board? Could it be that *Elohim* was upset with *Him!* May be the storm would cease if we did that and then we could be safe!

"Master wake up!" Someone cried! *"There is a storm and we have to abandon the boat! Wake up now and save yourself!"*

Another flash of lightening, and I see the Master standing at the bow, his hands stretched out. . .through the laughter of the demonic howl and the peels of thunder and flashes of lightening, a voice spoke!

No, a voice thundered! *"You wind and you storm. Be muzzled!"* *I had never heard that tone of voice before!*

It was a voice that rose above the cacophony of the wind and the crashing waves and grabbed hold of my fearful and trembling heart! It was a Voice that seemed to echo past the sea and reach into the war room of *Ceres* and *Neptune* and *Zeus!*

It was the Voice that had spoken in the first book of Moses. It was the voice of the I AM!

At that instant, the storm ceased; the winds died, and the clouds were pushed away!

I was terrified. It was better to have been in the presence of the storm than to be in the Presence of the One who can command the forces of nature to cease their activity!

Never in our religion, or history has any such thing happened before. True, Moses experienced God in the fire and earthquake and the wind on Mt. Horeb. True, Elijah was caught up in a whirlwind! But they did not tell the forces of nature, *"to be muzzled!"*

Throughout the course of three years, I had so much to learn about this *Man,* who could talk to demons, order nature to cease its deadly storms, give sight to the blind, and raise the dead from the caves of death!

But today, I am speechless! *Who is this Person? Is he God?*

I leave you with one thought. When He is in the boat, you have nothing to worry about! Just wake Him up! Talk to Him, and He will calm the worst moments of your life.

Via Maris. The Sea of Galilee and a tiny little boat caught in a storm!

That day, I knew I was in the Presence of the Creator God!

****

5

Two Demoniacs

δυο δαιμονιζομενοι

*When he arrived at the other side in the region of the Gadarenes
two demon-possessed men coming from the tombs met him.*
Matt 8:28 (NIV)

"*Filthy Canaanite dogs!*"
*We despised them as much as we hated the Romans! We
had had a longer history with the Canaanites than with the Roman
dogs! Moses and Joshua were both ordered by the I AM to erase the
Canaanites from the face of the earth, for good reasons! But they
didn't, did they? Instead they married off their sons and daughters
to these people who worshiped the Baalim.*

*These Canaanites worshipped Anat, who was the mistress of the
Canaanite gods, and she protected Baal. She lived in the underworld
and guarded the secrets of all the Canaanite pantheon! How about
Athirat? This god had seventy children, and she lived in the shores of
the sea. These gods married their sisters. Sisters became wives and
mothers became nursemaids. Brothers married sisters, and mothers
married their sons! Fathers married their daughters. And Baal? This
god lived and rode in the clouds and used thunder and lightning to
intimidate his worshippers! And during the dry summer months, he*

> *There was a blood curdling cry.* We stopped in terror! We knew what that noise was. It was the *demons*. Words cannot tell you what I witnessed. I stood my ground right behind the Master. This was the only safe place.

lived in the underworld! And how about all the rest of the hundreds of gods that they worshipped? Shapsu the sun-goddess, Yarikh, the moon god, Ashtar, the god of the desert, Shegar, the cattle god. . . .The system was so twisted and their worship was so convoluted! We had no business entering this unclean and unholy land, period!" I mumbled to myself as we got off the boat.

Look at what they produced! Swine! Pigs! That's right. They specialized in providing pork! The law that the *I AM* gave to us through Moses (PBUH) specifically stated that we should not touch or even be in the presence of the Canaanites.

And the *swine?* It was obvious that these pigs were being raised for the Roman pigs! Who else ate these filthy, dirty animals other than the filthy, dirty Romans that festered this peaceful land! Not just ten or twenty pigs! But a whole herd of them, two thousand, to be accurate, grazed the green hills on this cliffside!

What were we doing here? Did the Master *lose* his bearings after the storm? Even the air that is blowing in this land was thought to be unclean and possessed!

We should not be here and neither should He!

Incidentally, does not the Master know that there were demons that walked this part of the lake? No one, not even the local people, came to this part. It was rumored that there were demons in the form of humans that patrolled this part of the lake. Not only was this an unclean area, it was demon possessed. It was hell, in the literal sense of the word. It was the dominion of *Beelzebub!* The lord of the flies!

No one in their right mind came to this place!

But, here we were! I knew that it would only be a matter of time before all hell broke loose! I wanted to head back! I'd rather face the storm that we had been through just a few minutes back! I'd rather face the wrath of the Roman gods and be in the presence of *Zeus* and *Ceres* and *Neptune* than in the haunt of living demons.

There was a blood curdling cry. We stopped in terror! We knew what that noise was. It was the *demons.* Words cannot tell you what I witnessed. I stood my ground right behind the Master. This was the only safe place. Then I saw them: there were two of them. These two demons were naked; remnants of old rusty chains clung to their bleeding, ripped up legs. Their bodies were cut and bleeding. Their eyes were blood red and their hair was long, dirty, matted, and filthy. They did not look like human beings.

They were the embodiment of evil in the flesh!

They raced toward us with bone-chilling cries, their chains rattling and clanking on the rocks! Their screams of uncanny sounds that could put the fear of the gods into the most courageous zealot amongst us escaped through their foaming and contorted mouths. Their hands were clawing the air in front of them, and their eyes seemed to flash with a strange red luster!

I knew we would be killed by these demons. They would tear us to a million pieces! The rest of the disciples were already in the little boat, yelling and gesturing at the Master to run and flee from the demons and to join them.

But there He stood. Calm as ever, with the same calmness He had showed just a few moments back when He commanded the storm to *be muzzled!*

"We got nothing to do with you Jesus, ben- Elohim! Why are You here? Have You come to torture us?" the demons hissed and clawed at the air in front of the Master's face. I could smell their fiery breath and feel the sprays of saliva on my face, as they grunted at Him.

Did I hear this right?

"Jesus, ben- Elohim?"

Wait a minute! Hold on! He was *Jesus, ben Yosef!* NOT *ben-Elohim!*

And besides, to claim that God was your Father was a crime punishable by death.

And the demons were claiming that he was the *Son of the Most High!* This is blasphemy! That title was not even given to Adam who was truly the Son of God. Here were these two demons hissing at the Master and calling Him *ben-Elohim!*

Did these demons know some strange secret? Did this Man who stands before me exist once in a realm of the demons? Was there a war in heaven in which this Son of God fought the demons and won?

He did not say a word! Nothing! Not a single word! I expected a barrage of words to fill that graveyard! But no! Not a single word!

He just stood his ground and stared back at them.

Once again they both hissed in unison!

"See those pigs way in the distance?" they grunted in deep unison. *"Give us permission to possess them. . ."*

A single command came from the mouth of the Master:

"Go!"

That was it! It was the command that these demons had been waiting for! They slammed the two men to the ground, and it seemed a great wind rushed toward the edge of the cliff where the swine were peacefully sleeping! The demons possessed them and drove them right over the two-thousand foot cliff into the sea itself!

Incredible! I had never seen anything like this!

Two healed demon-possessed men and a herd of dead pigs!

Well, the pig herders ran to the village, and in a matter of a few minutes, a mob of angry people from the village approached us with sticks and stones and axes!

No one cared that the Master had healed two men! No one cared that there were now no demons that patrolled the hillside! They wanted us to leave the area at once!

It was ironic that the demons *begged* Jesus to send them away to possess the pigs and this mob from the village *begged* Jesus to leave them at once!

Ungrateful heathens! I told you we should never have come to this Canaanite village!

I want to leave you with this one thought! I was with the Master for three and a half years! The only time I heard him being addressed as *Jesus ben-Elohim* was by a pair of demons in a graveyard of a long-lost Canaanite village surrounded by unclean pigs! And Oh yes, I almost forgot: and a Roman centurion who oversaw the crucifixion!

No wonder it is said that he came to us and even we, the chosen *benim-Avram (children of Abraham) could not recognize the ben-Yosef who was really ben-Elohim, the Son of the Most High God! We needed the confessions of the demons to remind us who this Person was!*

How tragic!

It was a quiet ride back to Capernaum on the boat! No one, not even Peter the loud mouth whispered a word!

6
The Paralyzed Man

παραλελυμενος

*When they could not find a way to do this because of the crowd,
they went up on the roof and lowered him on his mat through the
tiles into the middle of the crowd, right in front of Jesus.*
Luke 5:19 (Matt 9:1–2) NIV

This is crazy!
I didn't know that there were so many sick people in our town!
Where did all these people come from? I thought I was the only one
who was *sick*. You see, I was a paralytic, cursed by God Himself! My
legs were shriveled up! They looked like the sticks that the camel
drivers used on their camels! It had been a long time since a disease
with no name possessed me and the nerves in my legs slowly and
gradually died! It was my wild lifestyle and the number of "friends"
that I had visited in my younger days!

In our society, if you are sick, you have been cursed by God, and
if you are wealthy, you have been blessed by God, praise be upon
Him! The Rabbis often quoted Dt 28:22,61: *"The Lord will strike
you with a wasting disease. . .The Lord will strike you until you are
destroyed!"*

Fear was the motivation for serving this God!

> I had no choice. I was at the mercy of some kind friends who loved me and did not respect my wishes! *They saw beyond me. Their faith overcame my despair. Their hope drowned my unworthiness! Their love destroyed my burning hopelessness!*

Look at Noah and the flood! Couldn't God have saved more than just eight people? The *Tanakh* said that He even destroyed the fish, because they were sinful!

And oh yes. . .how about the angel of death going about *Mizraim* in the middle of the night choking the throats of the innocent Egyptian firstborn!

How could you not remember Korah and his family. . .just because he disagreed with Moshe?

And Nadab and Abihu and Samuel's sons!

Ah Yes! Sodom and Gomorrah! *"You obey Me. . .or else I will kill you!"*

How about Judah's firstborn! Er. . .look it up yourself, it says that Er was wicked and YHWH *slew* him!

I mean, look what happened to Miriam, Moshe's sister! She spoke against the prophet Moshe, and she was *struck* with leprosy.

The people grumbled in the wilderness and, yup! Plagues and death and snakes and scorpions!

Look at Uzzah; he touched the ark of YHWH and he was struck *dead* by God Himself!

I did not stand a chance! In my younger years I had been wild. I had run with the rough kids in the neighborhood and had done a lot of things I was not proud of. One day my *sins* caught up with me and I got sick, real sick. I became both physically and mentally sick!

Have you ever experienced something like this?

You do something bad, and while you are doing this, you are enjoying *it*! Then just after you do *it,* you are afraid that God is going to punish you for this thing that you did! You start blaming yourself and how stupid of you to have done this! You wait for the wrath of God to come on you! Because you know that deep in your heart what you did was a total sin, with a capital "S!" You couldn't care less about the pleasure at this point. What seemed to be such a *pleasurable* experience becomes the grave that you have dug for yourself. You just want to get out but you can't! You are trapped!

The devil not only *led* you into this sin, but he now talks to you and tells you that God is going to destroy you for committing the sin. He even uses the words of the *Torah* to crush you! You just can't win! You withdraw. You slowly waste away.

Somehow after a few days you climb out of this *grave* you have dug for yourself *until the next time!*

The sin becomes a vicious trap, and slowly but surely the devil begins to tighten that noose around your throat, and you have nowhere to run! You know you can't run to God because the devil keeps telling you that you are a *sinner*, and God hates sinners! The walls close in until you are completely entombed in self-pity, frustration, mental anguish, and despair. Many a sleepless night you contemplate ending this life! *If only I could walk, I would end this life!*

That was me!

Physically and emotionally I was a paralytic. Some strange disease had taken over me, and now my nerve endings were gone. My mind was totally destroyed! I was afraid of God! I knew that I was a total sinner and that soon, I would be *struck dead* by God Himself.

My faith in life was gone! I had a few good friends. You know, the kind that came every so often and visited with you and told you jokes, but no one talked about the camel in the tent! My sickness! They knew I was dying. I knew I was dying! We all knew that God was slowly but surely killing me!

And the devil had scored. He whispers, *"God can't help you! You are the worst sinner in all Judea! He hates you! You are worthless! God will destroy you!"* Such words would lull me to sleep and my conscience would haunt me all night long.

My body had wasted away. My mind was tortured constantly.

"Where are You, God! Just strike me dead NOW! Put me out of my misery and take my life NOW! I cannot handle this any longer!"

"We are going to take you to see this Miracle Worker." The door to my hut flung open, and four friends of mine entered my filthy hut!

"You remember Shlumiel, that lame beggar that used to sit in front of the synagogue? Well, guess what happened? He went to the

Miracle Worker and He healed his leg! Also that blind beggar Tovit, who used to beg by Meshulam's bread shop? Guess what, he went to the Miracle Worker, and He gave him sight! Look, the Rabbi last Shabbat said that only God can heal a blind man and make the lame to walk! We are going to take you to him! You are no worse off than Shlumiel or Meshulam!"

That is the *last* place I wanted to be! If this miracle worker was sent by God Himself, I do not want to see Him! It's like the straw going to meet a blazing fire. God was angry with me for committing all those *sins,* and if He found me, I would be dead. Even *Moshe the prophet* could not approach the burning bush, and all those people that touched Mt. Sinai got killed. If God is in this land, I sure don't want to see Him! Even though I am a paralytic, at least I am alive! *I do not want to DIE!*

"No, I don't want to go! Let me just stay here!" I whimpered!

You see, when you are at the mercy of others, you have no choice!

I was sick! I was dying! I was a paralytic! I had no choice. I was at the mercy of some kind friends who loved me and did not respect my wishes! *They saw beyond me. Their faith overcame my despair. Their hope drowned my unworthiness! Their love destroyed my burning hopelessness!*

They carried me out the door in my bed, past the bread shop, past the town square and the market, and in front of a crowd of sick people seated on a grassy knoll! They laid me under an olive tree! It had been such a long time since I had felt the warm sunshine and the cool breeze from the sea and the velvet touch of the gentle green grass! I could see a blackcap warbler perched on the tree. It seemed I had entered heaven itself!

Ah! Here was that voice again! *"God can't help you! You are the worst sinner in all Judea! He hates you! You are worthless! God will destroy you!"* This was reality. In desperation I shut my eyes and hoped for death!

I heard them mumbling something and conferring with one another. The crowd was large and packed inside a house, and He was *inside* the house. They could *NEVER* get inside that house, not with a bed! Finally, I can be taken to the solitude of my house. I wanted to see no one and meet no one and. . .*Let me be!*

Then these friends of mine did something totally unexpected! They carried me to the roof of the house inside which this man was preaching. That's correct! You heard me right! *They carried me to the roof, their feet poking holes in the thatched roof!* A few more steps like this, and the entire roof would collapse. Four men and a sick man on a bed on top of the house: people were calling out to us and shouting at us to get down from the roof! I think it was the owner that was brandishing a stick and screaming at us in some colorful Aramaic! And then they started to tear open the roof! I couldn't believe this! These friends of mine were crazy. They were ripping apart a perfectly normal roof! They were making a hole in the roof! They opened the roof of the house! The grass and rocks and dust were falling all over those seated inside the house. My friends didn't care, which was comical! They didn't really expect to send me inside the house through the roof, or did they? They then tied some ropes to my makeshift bed and lowered me right in the middle of the house with all those people covered in dust! I thought these people would surely kill me! I was at the den of angry lions, like Daniel! The people, the owner of the house, and God—all mad at me! This is the last place I should be. All I could see from my bed were the faces of these friends of mine and a hole on the roof of the house! They were determined to get me to this Miracle Worker, even if it meant that they would destroy a perfectly normal house. Nothing came between them and their mission. They would get me healed, whether I liked it or not!

I wish I had some of their complete and insane faith!

His Voice broke through my thoughts like the shaft of light that pierced through the hole on the roof of the house, illuminating the dust and the debris that was floating in this overfilled room of sick and coughing people!

"Son, Your sins are forgiven!" I heard a voice say to me!

WHAT? My sins are forgiven? Wait a minute! Only God can give sight to the blind! Only God can make the lame walk! Only God can heal a paralyzed man! Only God can forgive my sins! At that moment the Voice filled my soul and reached into the darkest recesses of my troubled and desperate heart and wrenched out the box of catalogued sins that I had collected and visited time and again.

That Voice ripped my heart open and took that box and replaced it with forgiveness and faith; instant comfort and hope, thankfulness, joy, and peace swept over me from the bottom of my feet to the tip of my head!

My sins are forgiven by God Himself; I have no fear of today, or tomorrow!

"Take up your mat! Go to your house!" I did not need a second invitation!

Instantaneously I stood up, took my mat, and ran out that door! I was healed—just like that! I ran through the bewildered crowd and into the arms of my four friends who believed that He could heal me and had stood in the gap for me even when I could not see beyond the hopelessness of my desperate situation!

Years of pent-up guilt had dwarfed me! Years of fear of an angry God had stunted me until I had become a physical midget and a mental recluse. Only God could heal me! And He did! Only God could destroy the walls I was entombed in! Only God could raise my dead and hopeless soul! He saw the faith of my friends and my desperate state and took a chance on me and forgave my sins!

On the Shabbat, Rabbi Eretz read from the book of Isaiah:

"I, even I, am He who blots out your transgressions for My own sake and will not remember your sins!" Isa 43:25

Let me leave you with a final thought. What can I say? God forgave my sins that day! God healed me! God rewarded the faith of my four friends! That Sunday, we gathered new roofing material, and all five of us climbed the roof of that house and repaired the hole! It felt good to laugh, to joke, to feel the warmth of the sun beating on my back! The hole in my own life was patched by God and the faith of some friends who never gave up on me.

I deserved none of this!

This was grace. . .

7

Jairus' Daughter

ιαιρος θυγατηρ

While Jesus was still speaking, someone came from the house of Jairus, the synagogue leader. "Your daughter is dead," he said. "Don't bother the teacher anymore."
Luke 8:49 (NIV)

I am Jairus.
Let me tell you a little about myself. I am married. My daughter is a beautiful twelve- year-old girl with long black hair and deep brown eyes that look like the pools of Heshbon! She is the apple of my eye, and she is more beautiful than queen Esther herself! Whenever I got home, she would rush into my arms, throw herself at me, and all my troubles of the day would disappear the moment she whispered, *"Papa, I love you!"* My little girl was more precious than life itself. She was my world!

I am also the ruler of the synagogue. You see, the functions of the synagogue are divided into various sections. I was the *archisynagogos* not the *huperetes* of the synagogue.

Allow me to explain.

The *huperetes* of the synagogue is just the attendant of the synagogue. This person cleaned the synagogue, made sure that the

47

We entered the bedroom. There was my precious little girl! Dead! Her face was ashen, her hands cold! There was no breath! Death had snatched her away from me! How could God do this to me?

benches were in place, the scrolls were opened on the Shabbat, and made sure that the place was clean.

The *archisynagogos*, which was me, was in charge of the actual service of the synagogue. I was the president of the synagogue, the leader who in actuality was in charge of the entire synagogue. It was my responsibility to conduct the type of service, choose the prayers, choose the readings of the Torah for that day, and make sure that the right message was imparted to the people! We had specific readings for specific days and festivals. Ours was a system that was governed by tradition and guarded by rules!

My job was a huge responsibility and commanded respect and reverence. Think of me as a high priest of the temple! The responsibilities of the synagogue rested squarely on my shoulders! If the people had a spiritual argument, they would come to me, and I would explain to them from the *Torah*, the *Nabiim*, and the *Katuvim*. Along with my responsibility came great respect! You see, not many people in Capernaum could read the *Torah*. This was not Jerusalem, where the learned scribes and Pharisees argued loudly on the steps of the Holy Temple, which was guarded by temple guards and watched by sneaky spies! This was the quiet and rustic fishing town of Capernaum!

But we had a problem! *Jesus ben-Yosef!* He has been healing people and feeding them like Moshe did in the wilderness, and there was a rumor that he even silenced a storm over Lake Tiberius! The people were asking questions for which I had no answers. Too many questions, too few answers!

Was he *Elijah?* Was he another *prophet?* I was troubled. We had had no prophet that roamed the Galilean hillside for 400 years, and this *ben-Yosef* just explodes on this little sleepy fishing town! We all knew his parents *Yosef and Miriam*. They were just ordinary people, and there was a rumor that Miriam was pregnant before she married Yosef. And how could this Jesus be a *prophet?* Not likely! I wish He would just go away to Jerusalem! Let the scribes and the high priests there worry about him! I am an open-minded man, and the people respected me, and they wanted answers! I had none to give!

I was frustrated! I had my own questions and my own doubts! Too many crazy people have shown up, and it is my responsibility to guard and protect the people! I have to make sure! You see, the Romans kept political peace, and I kept the spiritual peace. Our society is riddled with superstitions and the miracles of the Almighty. It wasn't too far from here that Elijah had that encounter with Queen Jezebel and King Ahab! Our hillside was dotted with fables and stories from the Torah! It was here that the *chariots of fire* had appeared to Elisha.

I did not want to be accused by Isaiah the prophet, *"Israel's watchmen are blind, they all lack knowledge; they are all mute dogs, they cannot bark; they lie around and dream, they love to sleep!"*

Not on my watch! No way! I will guard my sheep!

Well, then, she got sick! The deep eyes, which were so beautiful once, became lifeless like the *Arabah, the dry wilderness! No laughter of a young girl greeted me each day!* My life was transformed from joy to sorrow in a moment! She only grew worse! I brought in all the physicians that I could muster with my prestige and popularity! These so-called "physicians" tried everything! They bathed her in therapeutic waters and gave her a multitude of medicines with myrrh, cinnamon, garlic, cloves, cassia, galbanum, and niter. Nothing worked! I think all those *"healing potions"* and ointments only worsened her condition!

I was desperate! Should I give in to the gnawing question that has been eating away in my heart? Should I ask *ben-Yosef?* What would the community say! If *ben-Yosef* healed her, then I would be forced to acknowledge that he was a prophet. Can I, as a ruler of the synagogue take that risk? What would Jerusalem say? If he couldn't and she died, I would be the laughing stock of the entire city! The vicious backbiting Jewish fishermen and their wives would tear me to pieces with their ridicule! What should I do? Thank the Almighty that she is at least not dead! If she died, only the Almighty could bring her back to life, and that I know is impossible!

Well, on one hand rested my reputation! On the other hand rested my daughter and the slightest chance that *ben-Yosef* might make her well! My reputation or my daughter; the choice was easy. My daughter came first!

I sought out *ben-Yosef!*

I begged him to come to my house and heal my little girl! He agreed! You see, wherever he went, there were crowds of sick people. He never bypassed anyone that came to him. I was in a hurry! He was stopping to heal some sick woman who had been bleeding for twelve years! Couldn't that wait? Doesn't he understand that if he did *not* hurry, my girl might just die? It seemed like he was purposefully slowing down.

Then my servant showed up! *"Master, she is dead. . .Don't trouble ben-Yosef!"*

It was all his fault! Had he hurried, my girl might just be alive. My whole world came crashing down on me! I looked for him! He was conversing with my servant! *"Take me to her."* he said, *"She is asleep! Let us go and wake her up!"*

Only God can wake her up from the dead, I mused! I was angry! Past the pressing throng, and past the bakery, and we were in front of my house! There were the wailers and the hired mourners! He just looked at them and said, *"Stop wailing. She is only asleep!"* These wailers simply laughed at Him! She was dead, and that was a fact.

We entered the bedroom. There was my precious little girl! Dead! Her face was ashen, her hands cold! There was no breath! Death had snatched her away from me! How could God do this to me? I had taken care of so many of His problems! Couldn't he have made her well? My only Tabitha! My precious little child! I would miss her hugs and her sweet voice! I would never hear her say, "Papa I love you!"

I felt like Hezekiah! "Remember now, O LORD, I pray, how I have walked before You in truth and with a loyal heart, and have done what was good in Your sight." Grant me the life of my child! Is that even possible! O death you have stung my old and quivering heart! Your darts have pierced me and left me bleeding in a pool of unanswered questions! Tears of anger found their way down my cheeks.

Would God even remember? Does He even care? Feelings of resentment drew their clutches around my throat!

Then I heard Him!

Jesus ben-Yosef was *talking* to my dead girl!

"Little child, Tabitha, get up!" His Voice cut through my wounded heart like a sharp Roman dagger!

I watched!

My precious little girl blinked her eyes once, twice, and drew a deep breath of that Galilean air and slowly, as if waking from a deep sleep she sat on her bed! There she was. She looked around, and her deep brown eyes locked onto my own tear-stained and bleary eyes as she threw her arms around me and whispered, *"Papa, I love you!"*

And what about *Jesus ben-Yosef?* He quietly melted into the crowd that had gathered in the front porch! He was gone even before I could thank Him!

I leave you with this one thought! Only God can raise the dead! Only God can talk to the dead and bring the dead back to life! To me he was not *Jesus ben-Yosef!* He is *Jesus ben-Elohim!*

Many years have gone by now. It all seems like a dream! My little girl is now married, and I am old and grey, and my own eyesight is not all that good, but my memory is crystal clear as the waters of the Jordan in the spring time! I can only tell you what I saw and witnessed. On a dark and gloomy Galilean day, many years ago, something wonderful happened in my house. God visited the house of a distraught ruler of the synagogue whose little girl was dead! My dead daughter was brought back to life!

The words of God would haunt me all my life!

"Little child, Tabitha, get up!"

****

8

A Twelve-Year Bleed

αιματος απο ετων δωδεκα

❦

. . .a woman was there who had been subject to bleeding for twelve years, but no one could heal her. She came up behind him and touched the edge of his cloak, and immediately her bleeding stopped.
Luke 8:43–44 (NIV)

*D*o you know how it feels to bleed for twelve years? I am constantly in pain! My garments are soiled all the time! I am continually embarrassed! I feel weak constantly. I am wasted and tired. I have no strength left in me! I am worried and tormented! I am always checking to see if I am bleeding, and I am a woman!

Rules! Laws! Regulations! If the disease did not kill you, the laws from the Torah sure did!

This is what the Almighty God had written and the Scribes made sure that the laws were obeyed!

A woman who bled was unclean, ostracized from those she loved, scorned at by those who she looked at, rebuked, forgotten—in essence she was walking dead woman!

"And every thing that she lieth upon in her separation shall be unclean: every thing also that she sitteth upon shall be unclean.

I had a plan! I would find out where he was going. I would wait for him, and when he came near me, I would touch just the torn, dirty edge of His garment!

And whosoever toucheth her bed shall wash his clothes, and bathe himself in water, and be unclean until the even. And whosoever toucheth any thing that she sat upon shall wash his clothes, and bathe himself in water, and be unclean until the even. And if it be on her bed, or on any thing whereon she sitteth, when he toucheth it, he shall be unclean until the even. And if any man lie with her at all. . .the bed whereon he lieth shall be unclean. And if a woman have an issue of her blood many days out of the time of her separation, or if it run beyond the time of her separation; all the days of the issue of her uncleanness shall be as the days of her separation: she shall be unclean. Every bed whereon she lieth all the days of her issue shall be unto her as the bed of her separation: and whatsoever she sitteth upon shall be unclean, as the uncleanness of her separation. And whosoever toucheth those things shall be unclean, and shall wash his clothes, and bathe himself in water, and be unclean until the even." Lev 15: 20–27 (KJV)

Everything she lies on, sits on, touches, is UNCLEAN!

I was unclean for twelve years! Twelve years in solitary confinement! Do you know what that means? You can't touch a person or be touched! You can't visit another member of the family. You can't have any social experiences! I don't think you even know what that means? Do you?

You cannot hold your grandchild, that cuddly bundle of joy! You can't even go shopping at the local market! You can't visit, talk, touch! You might as well be dead! For twelve long years I was dead to the world! I was a social outcast! You couldn't eat the Passover or be a part of the Shabbat meal! You could not participate in the full moon festivals or the *Purim!* It was twelve years ago when I last

53

celebrated the *Rosh Hashanah, Yom Kippur, Sukkot,* or the *Pesach* with my family. You see ours is a very social community! We loved our families and the family gatherings during these days of festivities. I did not belong in my own family! I was an outcast. A social misfit! It had been years since I enjoyed a Shabbat blessing in the synagogue!

I sought help from the best Roman, Egyptian, Babylonian, and Greek physicians. The Jewish physicians refused to touch me lest *they* become unclean. These "physicians" gave me some potions and fleeced me of all my money! Those heathen dogs were no better than the Jewish physicians! My husband and my family forsook me. Not that they did not love me, but it was the *LAW!* I was worse than the lepers who lived in the caves above the sea!

Years of pent up disappointments and broken promises and seclusion has made me calloused to any form of kindness. People abused me. . .shunned me. . .falsely accused me. . .They whispered that the hand of YHWH Himself was against me. I was a walking dead woman. No hope!

It was then that I heard about this Miracle Worker. Some said he was Elijah. Others said that he was one who was blessed by the Gods! Maybe, just maybe, if I could get near him and just touch him, I might be made well! But I had to get *near* him! Everybody in Capernaum knew me, and *if* I touched anyone, they could stone me!

I had a plan! I would find out where he was going. I would wait for him, and when he came near me, I would touch just the torn, dirty edge of His garment! That should do it*! I will stalk him for that perfect moment in time!* Then when He least expected it, I would touch that garment and melt away into the crowd. There is always a crowd around him, and no one would even know I had touched him! Just think, *IF* this miracle worker who was a rabbi knew that I touched him, he would become furious! He would be contaminated and *he* would have to go through all the purification rites written by Moshe!

This was my only hope. My only chance in my life!

I was desperate! I stalked him for days!

He was unpredictable! One day he would be by the seaside, the next day on a boat. The next day he would be in someone's home!

It was as though he was desperately searching for someone. I was getting frustrated! But I determined in my heart that I would touch the fringe of his garment. My life had a purpose. I was beginning to enjoy this!

If only *He* knew! I chuckled to myself.

That day I heard that he was heading out to the house of the ruler of the synagogue to some meeting, probably. You know how these rabbis loved to argue the fine matters of the Law. Who cares! I just needed to touch that filthy, torn edge of the garment. It was unclean anyway. It had seen more dirt than a camel that had not been washed in a hundred years!

So there I waited, a bundle of hope and frustration! I saw the crowd *headed my way! O Almighty God, please do not let anyone recognize me! It would be the death of me!* I edged myself closer and closer to the crowd. It seemed that no one noticed me! How could this be? I am being pushed and propelled forward towards him! I see him! No one said a word. In a desperate hope-filled moment I reached out and touched the torn, dirty, filthy fringe of this man's garment!

I felt my body experience a shock! It seemed like the lightning from the Arabah was charging thru my sick body! I began to gasp and almost passed out! I knew I was made well. Now if I could just sneak away!

Not so fast!

He stopped! "Who touched me?"

The big fisherman spoke, "Master everybody touched you!"

"Someone touched me with a touch of faith!" He replied!

I could not keep silent any longer! He knew who *touched* him! I fell at His feet!

"Master," I said. "I was sick for twelve years! I was desperate! In faith I reached out and. . ."

"Daughter," He cut me short, "I know. Your faith has made you well. Go in peace!"

Just like that! No explanations. No long treatise. No questions. No elaborate discussions of my disease! No embarrassing query into my sickness. Nothing!

Just two little words. *"Shalom lahalak!" Go in peace!* I needed *peace* from this turbulent life style that had devoured my body! I needed to *go* to all the thousands of places and people and events and things I had missed all these years. I needed peace. I needed release!

I want to leave you with this one thought! When this Jesus entered my life, I was sick. I was abhorred and forgotten. I was torn and bleeding and suffering for twelve long, lonely and desperate years. He restored me and gave me peace! He made me well! If he can do that to me, He can do it for you as well.

Touch him with Faith! He will make you well!

9
The Two Blind Men

δυο τυφλοί

As Jesus went on from there, two blind men followed him,
calling out, "Have mercy on us, Son of David!"
Matt 9:27 (NIV)

We were blind beggars. *Meshullam* and I. We begged alone, but traveled in pairs. We got the system down. You see, if you sat together and begged as a pair, we would only get half of the take. But if we positioned ourselves in strategic places, say about 200 feet apart, we could fleece the people twice. Then at the end of the day we could share our "earnings!"

We traveled in pairs. This was so that if one of us stumbled, the other would act as support. And, of course, for security as well. It would be difficult to tackle two blind, angry men and take their "earnings." Capernaum was full of little thieves who would watch you all day and at the end of the day they would jump on you, beat you up, and take your money! We needed all the protection and the security we could muster.

The only problem was that we were BLIND!

Do you know what that means? You have no sense of time! You rely on your "other" senses to guide you! Your sense of sound and touch compensate for your lack of sight! You hear things that you

I don't know what happened! Creation flashed through my dead and empty eyes! Jabbing pure white rays raced through my empty sockets. I could not imagine what was happening to me! I began to see a face in front of me! How can I forget that Face! How can I describe that Face?

cannot see! You don't believe me? Now close your eyes for a minute and count all the sounds you can hear. Now close your eyes again and tell me which sound is the farthest and which is the nearest! Now close your eyes again and drop a coin in front of you. Now tell me what that coin was. Close your eyes again and have someone bring you some food. Now as you eat it, tell me what you are eating! *You see what I mean?* You can begin to differentiate between sounds, distances, foods, and money as the rest of the other senses take over your eyes!

Now keep them closed for forty years! That is what we were—blind, old, and tired! Two blind men who had learned to trust each other over the course of time! We begged and lived and traveled and fought and argued and protected each other! And yes, we would probably die together! But we did not talk about that!

The highlights of each day were to hear the sounds of the travelers who went through this town of ours! You see, we were blind but we were not stupid! People will discuss anything and everything in front of beggars, especially blind ones! *They think that since we cannot see, we cannot hear also!* Ha! We had nothing to do but to sit and beg and listen. We had all day to listen to all these talks and discussion that went on in the streets.

Some of them were juicy bits of gossip! Some of these you don't even want to know!

There were the Romans who spoke in Latin. The fishermen who spoke in Aramaic. The learned rabbis who discussed their *"findings"* in Hebrew. There were the Egyptians and the Babylonians and the caravan nomads who spoke in some strange languages. We heard them all! We could even understand the grunts of the camels, whether they carried heavy loads or just a small load. If they carried the heavy loads, we would cry out louder than usual because we could get these people who were wealthy to give a larger *"donation"* to our survival!

From the sound of the coins dropping on my tin plate, I could tell whether it was a Roman *denarius,* a Greek *drachma,* a Syrian *stater,* or a Jewish *shekel.* But the fact of the matter was that most of the time we would get the one cent Roman *assarion* or the bronze Jewish *perutah,* which was what the widows carried!

We could tell if there was a crowd approaching and whether the crowd was a silent funeral procession, a happy wedding procession, a group noisy children, or a traveler's caravan!

At the end of each day we would gather in a quiet place (which meant that there was no human activity, thus a safe place), and we would "count" our money and find out if we survived or not!

Begging was an art! Blind begging was an art only a few of us possessed. To survive as a blind beggar was a gift given by the Almighty God. I was gifted, and I had to work at it to fine tune this fine gift! Those who did not have this *"gift"* just died!

There was nothing unusual about this day. We decided to beg together. I was the more crafty one. My mind was always on alert. You had to survive in this business, and in order to survive, you had to be alert!

A few days back I heard some people having a fiery discussion about someone named *Jesus ben-David.* It was a very interesting argument, which ended in a fist fight! *These unruly fishermen and their tempers!* Well, anyway, the argument was over something this *ben-David* was supposed to have done. He was supposed to have healed someone! Now, that got my attention! And, hold on to your seats: *the person who was healed was a blind man, a man who was born blind!* Did I hear that right? *A blind man!* Well that was exciting! That group was arguing over the claims the rabbis made that this *ben-David* could possibly be another prophet that had been resurrected. Or maybe, just maybe, he was the *Messias* that was mentioned by one of the prophets; I think they said *Isaias!*

This was way over my head. All that I knew was this! There was a prophet roaming the streets of Capernaum, and he was healing people! Maybe I could be healed too? *I wonder what it would feel like to be freed from this bondage of blindness!* Whose face would I first see! There were no requirements to be healed. I don't recall anything about being a Jew in good standing as a prerequisite that this prophet required for a good healing. I had the right to a healing just as the next blind beggar!

The problem was that I had to find this prophet! How does a blind man find a person who he had never seen before? Even if my eyes were not blind, I would not be able to find him! Hmmm! That posed a problem, and I could not for the life of me wrap my head around that one! I couldn't ask the local people to *lead* me to the prophet! The Jewish law clearly stated that blindness was a curse handed down by YHWH Himself. *And* touching a blind man, just *touching* the possessions of a blind man would require extensive ritual purification! No wonder the people just threw their "donations" at us, lest they somehow became contaminated!

Hmmm! Oh well! There is no way on this earth that I, a blind man, would find this prophet. *Unless, God Himself directed the paths of the prophet to me! Unless God Himself came my way! That was very unlikely, since the same God of this prophet had cursed me with blindness!* I was hopeless! There was no hope. Trapped in this blind tent I would spend my days until death snuck on me. It was the truth and a painful reality.

I heard a commotion! A group of people praising and singing and dancing! Women, children, and men! The sounds woke me up from the pool of depression that I found myself drowning in!

"What is going on?" I shouted, hoping for an answer!

"Jesus ben-David is coming this way and he is healing people!" a voice of a woman answered back!

"WHAT?" My only chance in a lifetime is coming my way! "Meshullam, get up! Jesus ben-David is coming this way!" I told my blind companion!

We jumped up to our feet and shouted—no, screamed—at the top of our voice "Jesus ben-David have mercy on us!" We screamed at him again "Jesus ben-David have mercy on us."

That same voice answered back. "He is going into a house; I will take you to him!" I couldn't believe my ears! Stumbling falling, Meshullam and I took hold of the hand of this voice and were led into a house!

Once again I shouted, "Jesus ben-David have mercy on us."

I could not believe myself. I was in the presence of a prophet! I did not know whether He was near me or far away! I would make myself known to Him. This is my only chance!

Then He spoke, "Do you really think I can do this?"

I had no doubts! "Yes, Lord!" I blabbered back!

Did I just call him "LORD?" Oh! Oh! That meant stoning! I had just announced in front of all the people gathered here that Jesus ben-David was actually God! Not good! The whole house became silent! I knew that the mob would grab us, take us outside the town to the waste heap, and stone us to death!

I had declared a man to be King and God!

Silence!

I heard footsteps approach my condemned soul.

A pair of cracked, calloused, rough splintered hands touched the sockets of my empty eyes!

He spoke! "According to your faith let it be done to you!"

I don't know what happened! Creation flashed through my dead and empty eyes! Jabbing pure white rays raced through my empty sockets. I could not imagine what was happening to me! I began to see a face in front of me! How can I forget that Face! How can I describe that Face? I can't! How can I express colors and describe objects? Joy and exuberance filled a heart that was forgotten long ago by the dusty roads of Capernaum! I saw Jesus ben-David. No! To me he is Jesus ben-Elohim, the Son of the Most High God!

Meshullam and I were healed that day! Jesus told us to be quiet and not to tell everyone what had happened! He might as well have asked the sun not to rise the next day! How could you not tell the whole world? I guess you would not know! You were not blind once, or were you?

We became His voice. We spread the news, His news, all around the country. We told everyone who would listen how *Jesus ben-David/Elohim* healed us and gave us eyes to see!

I want to leave you with this one thought! The first face that I saw in my life was the *Face of God!* It is kind, patient, bears all things, hopes all things, believes all things, endures all things. It never fails!

I saw God! You can too! He will reward that tiny little bit of faith you have!

"Meshullam! Come on! We got work to do!" I shouted.

No longer beggars but evangelists of the King and our God!

10
The Mute Demoniac

κωφον δαιμονιζομενον

*While they were going out, a man who was demon-possessed
and could not talk was brought to Jesus.*
Matt 9:33 (NIV)

*D*ouble trouble!
Mute and demon possessed! Wow! One is trouble enough, but
being *"blessed"* with two of these! That must have been quite the
"disease!"

The rabbis taught that all sickness came from the demons and
curses came tumbling down from *YHWH* Himself! So this person
must have been doubly assaulted by the demons! This person, (let's
just call him *Midyan,* a Hebrew name meaning "strife, war") was
both deaf and dumb, hence mute! Can you imagine not being able to
hear and not being able to speak? Wow!

I could not help but wonder! *"What was the sin that led the
demons to possess him? What caused this person to stray away from
God? Was it his upbringing or was it a traumatic experience like a
death in his family that made him bitter and turn his back on God?"*

You see, every time Jesus healed a person, *and he healed whole
villages,* I would wonder whether that person who was once

afflicted would now return back to the *sins* he once committed or would he begin to lead a cleaner life? Were some of these healings absolutely pointless, with no resolution? What if these healings were a cyclical reversal— the person gets healed and he returns back to the same "disease" after a while and then, *Bam!* Seven more demons possess him! His condition now is worse than when Jesus met him!

> *I had so much to learn! Even my own personal life and upbringing would be transformed daily as I witnessed the miracles Jesus performed! He was compassionate! I wasn't! He was forgiving! I was judgmental!*

But who am I to question the acts of God!

As I am writing this I am more than ever convinced that Jesus is the Son of God! Who else could deal with us with such kindness and mercy? We are all equal in His sight. No one has an edge over another. He sees all of us as one people. True, He healed individuals. True, I have no "demons" within me. *Or do I? I am hateful, critical, judgmental, angry, uncompassionate, arrogant, foul mouthed, vindictive!* Come on! These are not attributes belonging to an angel! But slowly Jesus has entered my own personal life, removing the cobwebs and chasing out one demon at a time until I am so infused with him and possessed by Him that I would travel all the way to Africa to proclaim the resurrection story! *But this story is not about me, Matthew the tax-collector!* That would have to wait for another time and another place!

Today it is this deaf and dumb demon-possessed filthy excuse of a human being that is writhing in front of the Master who takes center stage! *Let's talk about his troubles!*

He was deaf! He could not even hear the *shofar!* We live in a society that depends on the hearing of the *shofar,* (the ram's horn call to worship) and maintains that unless you respond to that call and worship YHWH, you are doomed. He could not even hear that! The poor wretched soul was slated for the fires of hell. Regular prayer is such an integral part of our worship.

He was not even able to hear the words from the *Torah* on the holy Shabbat! How could he hear the words of Rabbi Eretz who so faithfully guided our community from pitfalls?

Oh, yes! How in the world could he hear the announcements made by the Romans or the sound of horses or carts or screams of warning or words of love? This poor miserable soul lived in a vacuum by himself! At least he could see!

He could not speak! Now that is scary! How could he voice his pain? He could not utter any *tefelahs!* (prayers). He could not even repeat the "Shemay!" *"Shemay Israel YHWH Elohinu YHWH ached." (Hear O Israel, the Lord our God is one God!),* which was such a crucial element in our worship. He wasn't able to confess his sins on the head of the Passover lamb! He wasn't able to get his sins atoned for! Or cry out with joy, or share his love with someone, or argue the fine points of existence, or shout words of offense at an enemy, or defend himself in a court of law, or ask for a cup of water on a hot Galilean night! He couldn't even join in the *hillal, couldn't even praise God for all the blessings!*

What blessings? Wasn't it God that had cursed him with this disease? In his silent world, God deserved no praise!

He was under the control of demons! Now that is easy! No worship. No atonement for sins. No praises. No confessions. No God. Yes, possession! $2 + 2 = 4$! Simple logic. He could not reach out to God and guess what? He became possessed! *Is that how God works?* In my mind that seemed a solid excuse and a proper argument as to why this man was possessed! I had so much to learn! Even my own personal life and upbringing would be transformed daily as I witnessed the miracles Jesus performed! He was compassionate! I wasn't! He was forgiving! I was judgmental! He was kind! I was vindictive! He was God in action! I was just a tax collector that needed to grow! *But wait! The story is about this demon-possessed wretched soul!*

What a wretched life! This man had the ultimate sickness. The perfect sickness, if ever there was such a thing! You can see, but you cannot hear! You can see but you cannot speak or warn or love or share or. . .Life had been cruel to him, and his God had forsaken him!

And here were these groups of people who had brought him to Jesus for a healing!

Did they really expect the Master to heal him? I had witnessed the Master heal people who had a single ailment. I had witnessed Him chase away the demons. But here in front of us lay this miserable excuse of a human being; writhing in a contorted manner, foaming in his mouth, eyes bleary like one that had indulged in some cheap palm wine from *Nabatea!* He was trying to say something as he was squirming on the ground! *Growling, spitting, hissing, half human half animal!*

The Master just looked at him, full of compassion and mercy and forgiveness! God was kneeling beside His distorted creation! He knelt beside him as this madman tried to squirm away from Jesus. The farther he moved, the closer the Master came. The Master had backed him right against the wall of the house! The man could retreat no further! The man began to utter some strange and weird squeals of confusion and pain and clawed the air in front of the Master's face!

The Master sat beside him right on the dirt and held his hand. He took hold of that matted, bearded dirty face that had not been touched by anyone since the day his mother birthed him in some long forgotten Judean hut, and with a voice that was barely audible, the Master whispered, *"Be gone! Be healed!"*

I could not believe the instant transformation that took over this miserable man!

With sobs of gratitude and words of praise, this man, who was just a few moments ago an object of torment and evil, reached out and threw his arms around Jesus! It was an embrace of gratitude and thanksgiving! He was perfectly made whole! He could hear! He could speak! He was possessed by the Spirit of the Creator of the universe!

Radical, instant change!

Let me leave you with this one thought! The Master transformed one soul at a time! One wretched miserable demon possessed soul at time! As I was witnessing these miraculous events, He was transforming my own personal life. Come to Him; he will transform your life too! One life at a time!

That evening, under the starry skies, somewhere in the hills just above Capernaum, there would be one more son of Abraham who would be praising God for His intervention and deliverance in his life and for restoring him to the Image of God! And the Image of God that was once the Word and existed in a realm without time, disappeared into the darkness of the night in search of another son of Abraham held in the clutches of the evil one!

And I, a tax collector, was being transformed by the same Word that had healed this wretched mute demoniac!

11
The Withered Hand

η δεξια ην ξηρα

*On another Sabbath he went into the synagogue and was teaching,
and a man was there whose right hand was shriveled.*
Luke 6:6 (NIV)

Y om Shabbat! The Sabbath Day!
YHWH commanded Moshe to write, *"Remember the Yom
Shabbat (Sabbath day) to keep it "qodesh" (holy). Period! No
questions asked and no way around that! Just a simple command:
"Keep it holy." Now, that is difficult! How do we keep the Shabbat
"qodesh,"(holy)?*

This day was blessed and hallowed by the Creator God, and *He*
even rested from all His works! Therefore, we worshipped God on
His holy day! Anyone caught *breaking* the Shabbat intentionally or
"accidentally" was to be stoned to death according to the laws of
Moshe! You don't believe me? Read it yourself!

> ~~And while the children of Israel were in the wilderness, they
> found a man that gathered sticks upon the Sabbath day. And
> those who found him gathering sticks brought him to Moses and
> Aaron, and to all the congregation.

Jesus stopped in front of this man! The synagogue became deathly quiet! The rulers of the synagogue and the scribes and the Pharisees approached Jesus. They were like vultures waiting to pounce on an innocent lamb.

And they put him under guard because it was not declared what should be done with him.
And the LORD said to Moses, The man shall be surely put to death: all the congregation shall stone him with stones outside the camp.
And all the congregation brought him outside the camp, and stoned him with stones, and he died; as the LORD commanded Moses. (Num 15:32–36,32)

That was just one incident! This man was only gathering STICKS! And we the children of Israel stoned him to death! What if the poor wretch was gathering wood to light a fire to keep him and his family warm or cook some food so that his family did not die from hunger, or what if he gathered the fire wood just so that his poor wife or his children did not have to! *No! Nothing matters!* We just quoted the Torah, took him outside the camp, confiscated the contraband, and *stoned* him and left his wife without a husband and his children without a father. . .But we "fulfilled" the demands and the regulations of the Shabbat! I don't understand that logic! Do you?

Well, the rulers and leaders of the synagogue and the temple guards were on extreme alert on the Shabbat day! If anyone, I mean *anyone,* broke the Shabbat laws, God forbid, they were dispatched immediately, without prejudice. There were no exceptions!

So in order to help us understand the Shabbat better, the rabbis and the Pharisees got together and made laws about Shabbat observance. They called them the *forty minus one* laws. These regulations further became the launch pad for thousands of minute and minuscule laws called the *halach* or the way of life!

A few examples would help us understand this better!

A tailor could not carry a needle in his pocket on the Shabbat! If he touched the needle on the Shabbat, that would be a sin because he would have touched the tool of his trade, which would constitute "work!" Thus "fences" were made on the Shabbat to make sure that no one violated the Shabbat! Women were forbidden to look in the mirror, lest they see a white hair and inadvertently "worked" on the Shabbat by removing one of the white hairs!

You might think that these laws are crazy. But you see, for 400 years there had been no prophet who had walked the streets of Jerusalem, and the priests decided to protect the laws and thus the reason for some very astute and stringent laws! And for 400 years these Shabbat laws became a key element in our daily activities! If the local rabbi did not understand the law, he would explain it to us the way he *thought and understood* that particular segment of the law! Thus there were spins and confusion regarding the Fourth Commandment! It varied from synagogue to synagogue. Even the rabbis at Capernaum could not agree with the rabbis in Nazereth, just a few miles away! However, these *laws* were religiously enforced! Crazy!

And here on this holy Shabbat, we were seated in the synagogue, listening to Rabbi *Jesus ben-Yosef* as he expounded the meaning of the texts hidden in the Torah! Mind you, we were sticklers for keeping the Law. The Shabbat was the most important day in our week and in our lives! It was YHWH's eternal sign! Read it for yourself! *"Keep my Sabbaths holy, that they may be a sign between us. Then you will know that I am the LORD your God." Ezekiel the Prophet wrote in the Nabiim!*

So here we were seated in the hearing of *Jesus ben-Yosef,* and he began to read to us and to expound on all the little nuances of meaning in a way that only He could. It was refreshing! He made so much sense. The meeting was over, and he was just about to leave when he stopped! He noticed someone. Someone in the back seat had caught his attention! He was looking directly at me.

There was our local crippled man who was sitting just ahead of me! Jesus approached him. He stopped right in front of him. My heart was pounding! I knew that He had healed people before and. . .*Oh! Oh!* I hope he would not heal him on the Shabbat! All eyes were on Jesus, including those of the synagogue leaders and guards. It was obvious that this man had a shrunken, shriveled up right hand. It was dried up! No muscles, no sinews, just a piece of bone housed in a jacket of dry crackled skin! Even his fingers were contorted and paralyzed! The right arm was shorter and stunted! It was useless! He might as well have gone to the local physician and had that arm chopped off. What good is a hand that cannot be used? He could not provide for his family, work the field, do masonry, fish, clean, hug his child—nothing! His hand was completely dried up like a date or a fig that had been left in the hot sun. Cursed by God, this man had survived the silent accusations of generational sins all his life!

Anyway, Jesus stopped in front of this man! The synagogue became deathly quiet! The rulers of the synagogue and the scribes and the Pharisees approached Jesus. They were like vultures waiting to pounce on an innocent lamb. One wrong move on this Shabbat day, *Yom Shabbat,* and you are a dead man!

Jesus spoke. His voice echoed through the hallways of the synagogue: " *Young man, get up. Come and stand in the center!*" My heart was pounding!

I was right behind this man and I almost stood up! The command was everyone. Not just for this wretched soul.

The man stood up beside Jesus. Jesus put his arms around the sick man and thundered, *"Should we do good on the Shabbat? Or should we just destroy life on this holy day?"*

Well the answer was obvious, but where was he going with this logic? Of course you want to do good on the Shabbat. Didn't everyone know that? But what did He mean by that statement. *I hope he would not do what I think He is going to do!*

Jesus waited for an answer. The synagogue became deathly quiet! You could barely hear anyone breathing! It seemed like everyone was mesmerized or dead! There was a pregnant long pause.

Then He spoke, *"Stretch out your hand!"* You will not believe what I saw! That shriveled up excuse of a limb became full and vibrant! We all witnessed that hand grow and become a normal hand just like his other hand! It was a miraculous growth! It was like someone took that hand and blew into it. It gradually increased in size and stopped just as it became the same size as that man's other healthy hand! I saw it! I witnessed it! I am telling you it was pure magic!

The man was exuberant! The rabbis were furious! Not a single member from that learned group praised God for the miracle. All they were concerned about was their Laws and their observance. How dare this *ben-Yosef* violate the Shabbat observance right in front of them and in the synagogue in front of all these people! How dare he go against the Laws of the Shabbat! They were filled rage and anger, and they wanted Him dead! The whispers became noisy arguments mixed with accusations and words filled with disbelief and hatred at the same time! *I was dumbfounded!* Did Jesus risk his whole life to save a wretched man whose hand was withered up? Why risk the wrath of these synagogue rulers? The man could have waited one more day! It was not like he was dying, you know! Jesus could have waited till sunset! He could have asked the man to come the next day. Why did He break the Sabbath laws to heal the hand of a man who could have waited?

I want to leave you with one thought! Jesus could have waited till the Shabbat was over, and then he could have healed this man. He risked his entire life for that wretched sick man. *Why did He do that?* Then it dawned on me! He was on a mission! Touching one life at a time! And if I had been that man with a shriveled hand, He would have stopped to heal me as well, Shabbat or not! He would pass that way just once, and He would heal whoever requested His help! It did not matter if it was *Yom Reeshon or Yom Rebe-ee or Yom Shabbat.* The day did not matter, only the person did! *God was reconciling Man unto Himself, regardless of time, place, and location. This was the true meaning of the Shabbat!*

I was overcome with feelings as I saw the sick man rejoicing, the Pharisees accusing, and the crowd arguing! I did not know what I would have done had I been Jesus! But then, I am not Jesus ben-Yosef the carpenter's son from Nazareth! I simply shook my head and melted into the noisy crowd that had witnessed the healing of a man with a shriveled up hand and the open violation of the Laws of Sabbath observance.

(Note: Jesus would perform seven very poignant miracles on the Shabbat! And this would infuriate the rabbis so much so that they plotted to get rid of Him. How sad!

He would heal a lame man by the pool of Bethesda John 5:1–18;
He would drive out an evil spirit Mark 1:21–28;
He would heal Peter's mother-in-law Mark 1:29–31;
He would heal a man with a withered hand Luke 6:6;
He would heal a blind man John 9:1–16;
A crippled woman would walk again! Luke 13:10–17;
A man with dropsy would live to see another day! Luke 14:1–6)

****

12
Blind, Mute, Demon Possessed

δαιμονιζομενον τυφλον και κωφον

Then they brought him a demon-possessed man who was blind and
mute, and Jesus healed him, so that he could both talk and see.
Matt 12:22 (NIV)

Hang on to your seats, folks! Here comes one of the most
astounding miracles of all! This man had four counts against
him. He was blind, he was deaf, he could not speak, and he was
demon possessed!

Wow! Go figure this one out. How does one live? How does one
survive? How does one exist? If there was ever a soul that needed to
be made whole, it was this poor wretched man.

This is a very special miracle. In fact this is the *only* miracle of
its kind performed by Jesus that is recorded! He would not perform
this kind of miracle again. And incidentally, this is the only place
where Jesus would give the Pharisees an extended lecture about the
hierarchy of the unseen spirit world. He would in detail spell out to
the Pharisees the meaning of spiritual warfare.

We are all participants in this battle between good and evil, between God and Satan. *Some are destroyed, some give up and surrender, some lay bleeding in the battlefront waiting for the mercy of the grim reaper, and some are victorious.*

The only place in all scriptures and only I, Matthew, would record this incident! Not John, the beloved, or Dr. Luke, the physician, or the bright and energetic Mark. No one caught this except a tax collector who was saved by grace by the carpenter from Capernaum!

So let's plunge into this story shall we?

Fact: he was demon possessed!
Fact: he was blind!
Fact: he was deaf!
Fact: he could not speak!

He was a man who was imprisoned in the dark dungeons of hades, chained by the demons of hell, and guarded by Beelzebub himself.

He was unlike the two demoniacs or blind Bartimaeus or the mute man who could see! This character was locked up in the dwelling of demons, and the key to the dungeon was thrown out! Only God had the power and the right to claim him. Only God could reach out into that dark dungeon where this *ben-Avram* (the son of Abraham), who was created in the image of God himself lay wasting and dying.

This man was in the enemy's camp, not just in the camp of any enemy. He was guarded by none other than Beelzebub! Beelzebub was the prince of the demons; he was the head of all the demons. He was the *archon tou daimonion*. Some of the kings of Judah in the past had consulted Baal-Zebub, the god of Ekron. When king Ahaziah, the son-in-law of King Ahab, had fallen through the roof of the palace, he consulted this demon to see if he would survive or die! And of course, the famed prophet Elijah stepped forward, intervened, placed a curse on Ahaziah for consulting Baal-Zebub, and Ahaziah died, but not before fire came down and consumed the soldiers of Ahaziah twice, who had come to capture Elijah! What a story! So Baal-Zebub had a long relationship with the people of Israel.

There was even a following in our land where Baal-Zebub was worshipped. It was in the city of Ekron. The *writings* tell us that when the Ark of the Covenant was captured, it was taken by the Philistines to Ekron, the dwelling place of Baal-Zebub! Ekron was only a few miles north of Bethlehem, close to the sea! This was surely a war zone!

Let us look at the facts. Jesus, the Son of God, was born in Bethlehem, a few miles from the center of the home of the Prince of Demons. The Ark of the Covenant, which was the dwelling place of the Shekinah glory of YHWH, was captured by the Philistines; it was first taken to Ashdod, then to Gath, and finally to Ekron, the dwelling place of the prince of demons! The Shekinah glory, the prophet Elijah, the Prince of Heaven and the prince of the demons, all in close proximity!

Of course there would be victims of war.

Was it just a coincidence that Jesus invoked the name Baal-Zebub in this miracle, or could it be that this poor wretched soul was caught right in the center of a great war *between Jesus the Prince of the angels of heaven* and *Baal-Zebub, the prince of the demons of hell?*

What was so special about this wretched soul that meant so much to the demons and meant so much to the Son of God Himself?

What was it that was so unique about this man that the demons afflicted him not once but four times! We know nothing about his family or his lifestyle! We don't even know if he was a Jew or a Gentile! Or does it matter? We would be witnessing a war!

We are all participants in this battle between good and evil, between God and Satan. *Some are destroyed, some give up and surrender, some lay bleeding in the battlefront waiting for the mercy of the grim reaper, and some are victorious. Some are taken captive and placed in deep dark dungeons, and some are beheaded in battle. Some are lost and wander in confusion, and some just give up all hope.* Here was this wretched soul who was taken captive and lay wasting in the dark dungeons, blind and frustrated like Samson and guarded by the strongest demons. The demons had claimed him in this battle zone! They had won!

I could not help but think that this man must have been very special to God, someone like Samson or maybe like Job! Was there a time when this man was so much in tune with God, like Samson was? Was there a period in his life, when, like Samson, he destroyed the forces that came against YHWH God? Was there a time in his life when this man was the darling, the apple of God's eye? Was there a time when this wretched soul that was rotting away in the dungeons of his mind was the one soul that had stood up for God and had spoken for God?

Could it be that this man was so special to YHWH that God told Satan the accuser in the heavenly courts to test him, like he did Job? Could it be that this was a *Job gone wrong?* Could it be that he cursed God when he was faced by the demons of hell? Could it be that the demons singled him out, cast their nets around him, and slowly but surely drew him from the presence and the protection of the Creator God Himself and chained him to this dark and dismal dungeon? Could it be that he was once God's mouthpiece? Was a war waged over this soul, and this wretched man just gave up and lost the war? *I could not help but wonder!* Was he given a second chance? *Could it be that he was a composite picture of all of us?*

This man was blind, deaf, mute, and demon possessed, but *He could think!* Could it be that he cried out from the dungeons of his silent mind for God to hear him one last time and his silent cries reached the very throne room of YHWH Himself and in a fraction of a second, the Master entered the realms of the unseen! Michael, the prince of angels confronts Baal-Zebub the prince of the demons! No longer do the demons see Jesus as a mere carpenter; He is the Divine, God in action doing that which he does the best! Destruction of demons! I could see demons fighting in the spiritual realm, hissing and screaming, *"You can't have him. He belongs to us!"*

Could it be that when naked, bruised, and bleeding he lay, chained and tormented and filled with confusion and hopeless despair that this *ben-Avram, this son of Abraham, a child of the Promise,* summoned one last breath of prayer with all his energy and in agony cried to God Himself from the dungeons of darkness *"My God! My God! Why have you forsaken me?"* Could it be that that cry of pain and a request for deliverance reached the very throne room of YHWH Himself, and could it be that an immediate response was dispatched without any delay with *"URGENT"* stamped all over it? Could it be that He was so special to God that God missed him so much that He sent none other than the Word that became Flesh, none other than the Third member of the Trinity Itself, and none other than the prince of angels to fight the prince of demons, and could it be that His voice thundered through the darkness of the demonic *domain, "Enough! He is mine! I am going to unchain him today!"* Could it be that Jesus and His mighty army are on their way for a showdown, for a victory, for immediate release? War! But the battle was already won! I wish we had the insight to look into the realm of the unknown! But in retrospect, do we really need to? Would we even begin to understand?

How little we understand spiritual warfare! How stunted and dwarfed is our knowledge! All we see is a man who is blind and deaf and dumb and demon possessed! Jesus would heal him that day. His hand of mercy and voice of compassion would touch this miserable soul that was blindly groping in the haunt of demons!

Could it be that the same prince of the angels, who parted the Red Sea, and spoke to Hagar the mother of Ishmael by the dried up spring, and who commanded Abraham not to lay a hand on Isaac, and who appeared to Moses in flames of fire in the burning bush, and who strengthened Elijah in the desert on his journey to Mt. Sinai, and was present in the furnace with the three Jewish boys, and was with Daniel in the lion's den, and with Jonah in the belly of a whale, and with Gideon's 300, and with Joshua's soldiers facing the impossible walls of Jericho, and with David in the valley with Goliath, and with Elijah on the showdown at Mt. Carmel, would in person fight for the very life of this son of Avram? This man must have been special! Very special!

I was seeing the prophecy of Isaiah in action! *"The Spirit of the Sovereign LORD is on me, because the LORD has anointed me to preach good news to the poor. He has sent me to bind up the brokenhearted, to proclaim freedom for the captives and release from darkness for the prisoners..." Isa 61:1*

There it was! *"Freedom for the captives and release for prisoners!"*

I want to leave you with one thought! The story is about this man! It is a story that is a lot like our own personal story! We are blind, spiritually blind. Jesus gave us sight! We were mute, spiritually mute. Jesus opened our mouth and ears! We were demon possessed, filled with *anger, malice, backbiting, envy, jealousy, unholy thoughts and secret sins*. Jesus delivered us! We had given our allegiance to the prince of demons, but the prince of the angels was on His way to set us free. *What a story!* All I can tell you is that I am breathless as I write this story! It is a story of a million others just like this one poor wretched miserable soul, who was terrified, tormented, and was living in the flames of hell and in the haunt of demons, after whom the prince of angels went and waged a war, destroyed the prince of demons, and won! And like Hagar, this wretched soul would exclaim, *"You are the God who sees me, and now I have seen the One who sees me!"* No longer blind, mute, deaf, and demon possessed! *Free at last!*

If He would fight for this nameless man, surely He would fight for me.

Hallelujah! Thank you Jesus!

13
5000 Men and...

πεντακισχιλιοι

"Here is a boy with five small barley loaves and two small fish,
but how far will they go among so many?"
John 6:9 (NIV)

You worked for a day and you were paid 1 denarius! Let's see what things cost at the time of Jesus: 1 egg would cost 1 denarius. 1 chicken would cost 30 denarii. 1 pound of fish would cost 30 denarii. A hair cut would cost 2 denarii. A lamb or a goat would cost 12 denarii. And half a liter of the best honey would cost you 40 denarii!

So, if you worked for a day, the Romans paid you one denarius. If you were a Roman soldier, you earned 1800 denarius a year or 6 denarii every day. Now that was some serious money! So, even if you worked for 200 days, you could not feed this crowd that was sitting on the grassy slopes listening to Jesus. That was roughly a year's wages! It was absurd! *That is the whole point of this story!*

It was the Passover season, and there were multitudes of people from all over the fertile crescent who were heading to Herod's Temple in Jerusalem. Galilee and the cities surrounding the Sea of Galilee were filled to capacity with strangers and people who were

"Philip!" I was jarred from my day dreaming! *"Philip! Go get bread to feed these hungry people."* the Master's voice broke through my wandering mind! I almost swallowed the olive pit I was playing with in my mouth! We were broke! We had no money!

on a pilgrimage. Any miracle or strange occurrences would travel all over the world. They would be embellished and repeated a thousand times over as these pilgrims returned to their far-strewn cities and remote villages at the edge of the world! This is the setting in which this next miracle takes place.

There were approximately 15,000 people who had been following Jesus for a few days! Now, mind you, that is a huge crowd! No, it was a mob of people. They were there to witness more miracles. They came from all walks of life! Jews, rabbis, Greeks, Syrians, Phoenicians, Romans, beggars, royalty, men, women, children, families, the sick; *you get the picture.* Here is where the action was. Free entertainment and of course answers to multiple questions. They would observe Jesus and take the reports back with them and share them under the stars and over the campfire in some long-forgotten village tucked away in the remote parts of the earth! Some even said that He was the promised *Messias,* who had come to set them free from the Romans!

I wish he would just tell them to go away. This group of people only followed him for the entertainment! I was sure of that. There was a rumor going around that when the *Messias* showed up, it would be like *Moshe* and the wilderness. We would be fed, our diseases would be healed, our shoes would not wear down, and we would get rid of this Roman occupation. Israel and Judah would once again be a force to contend with as in the days of King David and Solomon! We had the temple that sly Herod had built. All we needed was a King like David! This *ben-Yosef* possessed all the qualities! He could heal, calm the seas, argue with the powers, be polite (except to the keepers of the law), and command demons to disappear! He could be the KING that would lead us all against these Roman dogs! I wonder if he could feed them manna from heaven! That is the only thing that was missing. If he could provide food and water for us, we would really make Him king!

"Philip!" I was jarred from my day dreaming! *"Philip! Go get bread to feed these hungry people."* the Master's voice broke through my wandering mind! I almost swallowed the olive pit I was playing with in my mouth!

We were broke! We had no money! The Master must be joking.

"You are joking, right?" I replied! *"Even if we worked for 200 days and got paid, which was unlikely in these hard and difficult times and used that money to buy bread, just bread alone, we would not be able to feed these people! Master, there are 15,000 people sitting in front of us!"*

Andrew came to my help. With a smirk on his face he joined in the discussion. *"Look what I found. Five barley pieces of bread and two small fish! I think they are sardines from the Sea of Galilee!"*

Yeah, sure! He was probably looking out for himself and stole a little boy's lunch! That thief! I mused! And besides, what can we do with this "discovery". . .that cheap barley bread and fish won't even feed me!

Then the Master said something very strange! *"Make the people sit down in groups!"*

I didn't know what He was up to this time! You could never second guess Him. He was always one step ahead of us.

There were times He said things that made no sense at all! Like that time we were in a deep discussion and He said that those in the graves will hear His Voice! *I mean, really!* How is that possible? How can the dead hear His voice? The *Torah* clearly stated that the dead know nothing and when you die, you went to sleep and woke up some time when the world ended! It was not in my heart to disagree with the Master. But it does not make sense! And I just kept all this to myself. Not John! He was always asking questions, and Peter was always arguing! And that Judas was constantly figuring out ways to make some extra money! Thomas was always doubting. And Andrew was always bringing strangers to Jesus! We were a ragged bunch that followed Him. But that is another story for another time! That would have to wait.

But for now, we raced around the 15,000 people like a camel whose tail got chopped off and told that mob of people that the

Master wanted them to sit down! You should have been here! It was a glorious mess. Strangers, Greeks, Romans, Phoenicians, the sick, the women, screaming children, and angry husbands—it was tiring!

We just followed what He said! Just sit down and be quiet! I liked doing that! I felt kind of important. I was the mouthpiece of the Master, and they better obey. No one questioned, no one argued. It was almost like a canopy of peace blanketed this mob of confusion! We ran back to the Master, huffing and puffing!

What next?

Little did I realize that what followed next would be told around 15,000 campfires for generations to come! It would be told from one house to another, from one village to another, from one country to another, and it would reach Herod's Temple in Jerusalem and make the high priests livid with envy and plot His death and our persecution!

What next? Simple!

He placed the pieces of cheap barley bread and the two sardines on the grass in front of Him and prayed, *"Barukh atah Adonai Eloheinu melekh ha olam hamotzi lechem min ha'aretz."* (*"Blessed are You, LORD, our God, Sovereign of the Universe, who brings forth bread from the earth."*). It was a simple prayer asking God's blessing on the food we are about to eat! As He prayed, the bread and the fish multiplied. I could not believe my eyes! Things were happening before my very own eyes! Bread and fish in abundance! Thousands of pieces of bread and thousands of tiny pickled sardines miraculously multiplied in front of our own disbelieving eyes! Who is this Man that could command food to multiply? Who is this that can provide food for thousands of people with just a few measly pieces of barley bread and some fish!

Could this be the *Messias?* My ecstatic brain danced around the concept that I might just be in the presence of One promised by the prophets! There was enough bread and fish to feed the entire Roman contingent that was stationed in Galilee and Jerusalem.

Do you know what this means? With power like this at our disposal, nothing can stand in front of us. When we go into battle and get hurt, He would heal us. When we lack for food, He would provide for us. When the enemy would surround us, He would unleash the forces of nature on them and destroy them! We would be invincible! These Roman dogs who had snatched our land from us would be destroyed in a twinkling of an eye, and we would be the mightiest of all nations; we would make Him King and the twelve of us would be princes. . .it was a wonderful thought!

He told us to pass the food around.

Pretty soon the people had eaten their fill. And the hills around Capernaum were resonating with the praise songs to YHWH. People were dancing and singing and were ecstatic.

"Ya-se Sahlom! Ya-se Shalom! Shalom Aley-nu Wa-qol Israel. . ."

resounded throughout the hills above the Sea of Tiberius as the evening sun slowly began to set and little campfires began to dot the hillside. The reflection of the stars in the sea and the sound of praises and exuberance mixed with the smoke of a thousand campfires was simply magical. It reminded us of Joshua and the soldiers camped on the other side of the Jordan, just about to take over the land promised to the descendants of *Avram! We were now unstoppable. We could walk on water! We were ready!*

Let me leave you with this one thought! I had so much to *unlearn!* It would be painful. Very painful! I wish I had seen beyond the miracle of the food! I wish I had understood *why* He did *what* He did. I wish I had not been caught up in the moment of exuberance! I saw only power and my own advancement. I wish I could have seen compassion and concern that the Master showed to these people who were hungry and were in need of a Shepherd. They needed a Shepherd, not a King! They needed someone to wipe their tears and void their fears. I saw a mighty miracle. But He saw a nation wandering, groping, hungry, lost children of *Avram, sheep without a shepherd!* This miracle would trouble me for years to come! Lost in the moment, I totally misunderstood His mission. If I had only known who He *really* was, I would have understood Him better when He walked amongst us!

My heart cries within me. . .

I wish I had. . .

I wish I had. . .

Signed,
Philip

14
The Ghost

ΟΤΙ φαντασμα εστιν

When the disciples saw him walking on the lake, they were terrified. "It's a ghost," they said, and cried out in fear.
Matt 14:26 (NIV)

Wish John the Baptist had not been beheaded in the palace
at Makarwa by Herod! How could that half-breed so-called
king do that? How could he give in to the request of a dancing girl?

Just a few days back that ugly Herod, the fat half-cast fake, the
so-called coward emperor, in a drunken frenzy, had beheaded the
Baptist's head and had given it on a shiny silver plate to Salome,
the dancing girl! All this happened in that opulent mountain fortress nestled just besides Mount Nebo where Moses was shown the
Promised Land! Herod had thrown a huge party and had made wild
promises in a drunken stupor!

Had John the Baptizer from the Jordan been alive, we would
have forced him to declare *Jesus ben-Yosef* as the next king of the
Jews! He could have anointed Him. Well, wasn't he the one that had
said something about Jesus being sent from God Himself?

We should have done it! We should have made Him king and
declared our allegiance to Him. *We should have found another*

prophet, any prophet—to anoint Him and should have blown the *shofar* to sound the announcement. *"There is a new king in Israel!"* If only we could have found a prophet, Jesus would have been King! The problem was that there had been no prophet who walked these dusty roads for over 400 years! Seems that God had written us off and had stopped visiting us, until now!

> *What was that? It was a strange and a scary phenomenon! An apparition! A ghost! Long flowing robe swirling in the wind. Its feet barely touching the water. It was approaching our boat!*

Well we blew our chances!

The people were ready, and so were we. There was no opposition. There were no rabbis or temple guards or those despicable Roman thugs that paraded in their fancy shiny clanging armor. The hillside was covered with thankful people who had just now received a dream meal of fish and bread provided from the heavens, and blessed by YHWH. *But why didn't the Master announce the fact that He was the Messias?* Could it be that he was *not* the *Messias? Could it be that he was just an imposter?* I mean *really,* the way he was acting, you would think that he was trying *not* to be noticed. What was he *thinking?* Did he really think that this miracle of providing food for the thousands would go unnoticed? There was even a group of those Galileans farmers and carpenters and zealots who were forcefully trying to make him King! Even Judas, that opportunistic, untrustworthy conniving, glory-seeking zealot suggested that this was the optimum time, and he was learned and could read and add! *Jesus didn't seem to care about anyone's feelings!* He just slipped out of the camp and melted into the night! We did not know where He disappeared off to! He said something about wanting to spend time with his Father! The only *"Father"* he had was dead! But he was always talking about God the Father as His Father! Maybe he was just wanting a little rest! Who knows! *And at this point I really don't care!*

But we had to cross over to the other side of the sea. So off we went in our little boat. We were upset, arguing and wondering whether he was really the *Messias*! We were confused! We had seen some very exciting things, but we were not sure of many things! We wanted to believe that he was the promised *Messias,* but he was acting completely opposite to what our understanding was, with reference to *who* this *Messias* and *what* he was supposed to do for us! He was supposed to destroy the Romans, but this *Man* is talking about loving the enemy, and doing good to those that abuse you, and going the extra mile, turning the other cheek, blessing those that curse you, giving your tunic to the Romans! *Nothing is making sense anymore!* I don't get this! Something was amiss.

We all were frustrated! We were arguing, gesturing screaming at the top of our lungs with some colorful fishermen language that would have stopped the ears of the Galilean ladies who visited the fish market! We were so engrossed in the happenings of this day that nobody, not even the *sons of thunder* noticed the deadly storm that was descending on us with gusto!

You see, we were focused on ourselves! All that mattered to us was ourselves and the state of pity and missed opportunities we found ourselves in! We did not seize the day! We had let a perfect opportunity of making Jesus the King of Israel go by. That moment was lost forever, and we had only ourselves to blame! How tragic!

Then, without a warning, without even a simple warning, the sea of Tiberius unleashed its fury upon our small boat! The sea became a cauldron of boiling, demonic whirlpool! The earth shook, the waves became enormous, and thunderous clouds descended on us as gale force winds picked up this small boat and tossed it like a piece of dry grass in the desert whirlwinds from the *Arabah!* Lightning flashed, and thunder rolled! Our boat was taking on water! *We were dead!* We would be joining the thousands of dead fishermen and the hundreds of boats that lay at the bottom of this sea!

Sunset to 9 p.m. was the first watch. 9 p.m. to midnight was the second watch. Midnight to 3 a.m. was the third watch, and 3 a.m. to sunrise was the fourth watch! When we left the grassy slopes and the 15,000, it was the first watch. The sun was barely setting in the west, and we had been in this sea for a few hours. *We had been fighting the waves and the storm and the wind for a number of hours!* We were tired. *It was now the fourth watch!* And the storm was not letting up! It was relentless in its pursuit. It was evil, and it seemed to us that Beelzebub, the prince of the demons and the ruler of the underworld was at the helm of this storm! This storm would destroy us. You see, we had learned that in the end, we were at the mercy of the elements, and this storm had no mercy! *We had been fighting this fury all thru the three watches—nine hours—*and now we were entering the fourth watch. We were beaten and tired. *There was nothing more that we could do. This was it!* In desperation we began to tie ourselves to anything that would and could float! Flashes of lightning and peels of thunder cracked just above our heads! It seemed that the gods were in a war just above us! Maybe Neptune was waging a personal war with Mars and Pluto! The Romans often said that the gods waged war over the sea of Tiberius. The whole hillside was dotted with graves and the haunt of demons. Rumor had it that the demons even haunted these waters! It almost seemed like we had entered the war room of the gods, and I truly expected to see the demons of hell walking the shores of this sea, throwing their fiery darts of destruction at the gods that lived in this sea! When you depend on the seas and nature as much as we fishermen did, you have to believe in the supernatural. We were superstitious!

What was that? It was a strange and a scary phenomenon! An apparition! A ghost! Long flowing robe swirling in the wind. Its feet barely touching the water. It was approaching our boat! Flashes of lightning cut through the howling wind to light up this shiny spirit form that had materialized from the bottom of the ocean and was approaching our boat with determination! We started to scream and cower in fright! This was the first time any of us had seen a ghost! We tried to row away from this specter, but our hands were numb with fear. We were frozen in time! It was our belief that if spirits appeared at night, they had come to snatch us into the world of the demons! We were petrified with fear!

Then the Ghost spoke! "It is I! Be bold! Do not shake with fright!"

It was the Master's voice. We recognized that voice! Who could forget that voice. It was the same voice that had just a few hours ago prayed and caused that miracle of bread and fishes. But Peter had to open his big fat mouth! He was the only one that had any courage left in him! "If it is really You, Lord, let me walk on the water and come to you!"

Really, Peter? Are you sure? Do you really want to go to that form that sounds like the Master? What if it was a ghost? Had

Peter lost his senses? I had my doubts about this big fisherman! He appeared to be our fearless leader and was always so overconfident! The Voice replied, "Come on!"

Peter stepped on the water and walked! It was a major mistake! As soon as he saw the waves, he began to drown! Oh! Oh! A scream that was louder than the crack of the loudest thunder escaped from the lips of this big fisherman! "Lord save me, I am drowning!" he cried, and the Master reached out and lifted him straight out of the waves! And together they walked hand in hand back to the boat!

As soon as the Master set foot on the boat, the storm ceased, and we were on the shore, safe and sound! He didn't rebuke the wind or the waves or any such thing. No words were spoken; just a glance at the waves!

Wow! What a day! First the news of the death of the Baptist, next the feeding of the 15,000 people, and now Jesus walks on water and calms the storm, and we almost lost Peter to the turbulent waters! I am tired and must get some rest.

But I must leave you with this one thought! From high upon the cliff, Jesus must have been watching us for nine hours before he decided to come down and help us. The fact of the matter was that when we had done all that we could to save ourselves and there was nothing more left to do, not a single thing, and when we lay at the mercy of death, the master shows up! Sort of like that lady who was sick all these years! Pride had kept us from focusing our eyes on Jesus! And he would have to allow us to go through all that trouble for nine long hours before He would intervene.

I would learn over the years that He simply waits until you invite Him! He never goes where He is not wanted! And when fear has shut your soul and you are left all alone, He would show up, time and time again. We should have asked Him to help us at the first watch, not at the fourth watch! You know what I mean don't you?

I just shook my head as I pondered the events of this day and slipped into the world of dreams and campfires and chirping sounds of crickets!

15
The Dogs

ΤΟΙϹ ΚΥΝΑΡΙΟΙϹ ΒΑΛΕΙΝ

"First let the children eat all they want," he told her, "for it is not right to take the children's bread and toss it to the dogs."
Mark 7:27 (NIV)

*T*he fact could not be missed.

It was quite a distance to Tyre from Capernaum, about twenty-eight miles, and to Sidon in the north, it would be around forty-five miles. That whole entire region was full of heathens and trouble makers. It was not a safe region for a band of Galilean Jews to be traveling in. In fact, Ekron, was a center of Baal worship, and that was not too far from Bethlehem!

Jesus traveled in search of this heathen woman! Isn't that so much like him? He would do the same over and over again. *God in action seeking out the frustrated souls howling in the dark!* Regardless of the danger that surrounded Him, He would place Himself in com-promised situations just to save another soul. The Bible is replete with such marvelous miracles. But we should not get ahead of this story! We have to savor every morsel, taste every crumb that falls from the Master's dialogue with this poor and forgotten woman!

> When you are totally devoid of all hope and when frustration, destruction, worry, and sickness confine you and eat away at your very soul and you have nowhere to run to and no one to turn to, it is then that the Master comes in search of you.

Jesus was tired and wanted a place where he could just disappear to. After all, He was human just like us, and He experienced all the frustrations, the physical toll, the lack of sleep and constant bombardment by the authorities. There was not a single place that He could just go to and *relax!* He was always looking to see who would stab Him in bright daylight. Even in the spiritual realm, He had to keep His guard up! He must have been exhausted!

He was tired of all the publicity, and the people were hounding him for just one more miracle and one more healing. Have you had that happen to you? You just wanted to get away from all of it and be a *nobody* for just a day? Mind you, Jesus was well known in the neighborhood! Both in the seen and in the unseen realm He was popular! It wasn't every day that a prophet appeared and it was not every day that God walked the streets of Lucifer!

He came to his own and his own did not receive Him. In fact the chosen people were planning to crucify Him! So, He went to the world of the Gentiles for a little rest and relaxation!

It is to the unclean *shepherds* that the angelic choir sings the Christmas songs. It is to the wise men from the East, the *magicians* that the star of Bethlehem appears! It is the *centurion,* a Roman pagan, who declares at the cross that Jesus was the Son of God! It is to the untouchable *Samaritan prostitute* that He declares that He is the *Messias!* It is the groups of *demons* who would time and again confess that Jesus was the *Son of the Most High!* Do you notice a pattern? While the *"chosen"* people of God, the seeds of *Avram,* plotted His death, the Gentiles worship him, and demons acknowledge Him! What a tragedy! Here was God Himself seeking refuge among some heathen. He had to disappear for a while. So he went into hiding in the land of the Canaanites!

She, on the other hand, had five strikes against her!

Strike one! She was a Canaanite. The Old Testament had very strict rules regarding God's people associating with these heathens. The second book of the *Torah* clearly commands the destruction of the Canaanites when Israel entered the Promised Land. But here, Jesus was finding refuge and shelter in the land of the Canaanites. Instead of destroying them, Israel compromised and protected them! Even the wise king Solomon had wives from the Canaanites! Compromises were only too common in the days of the kings! However, at the time of Jesus, the land of Canaan did not exist, only the people did! They were known to worship a free form of a cult that included *Baal, Asherah, Dagon, El,* and other gods. They were a spiritual horde of people who had temple prostitutes and sacrificed their children to *Baalim* and they did not worship the YHWH God of the Old Testament. The woman in this miracle was a Canaanite! Strike one! Incidentally, Matthew the tax collector states that Simon, one of the twelve disciples was a *Canaanite*. Could it be that the *"house"* that Jesus retired to, here in this rather remote northern part of Palestine, was the home of Simon the Zealot? We can only guess and speculate!

Strike two! She was a Greek! That would also mean that she worshipped some or all of the twelve gods in the Pantheon. It could be that she worshipped, *Zeus, Poseidon, Hades, Hestia, Hera, Ares, Athena, Apollo, Aphrodite, Hermes, Artemis, and Hephaestus*. The Greeks also believed in the healing of the mind, body, and spirit! And the question is gently asked. Who was it that was really sick? Was it this woman or her daughter or could we surmise that they both were sick? One physically and the other spiritually?

Strike three! She was a Syrian! They were the dreaded enemies of the Jews. They were the merchant kings of the *fertile crescent*. They controlled the trade routes from Damascus to Babylon and beyond! They cheated and trusted no one. Ruthless in their bargaining, they fleeced the Jewish economy! Each hated one another with equality. The Syrian merchants cheated the Jews, and the Jews in turn treated them with suspicion and hatred. There was no love lost between these two.

Strike four! She was a Phoenician. The Phoenicians were the seafaring traders who traveled the then known world and brought in spices from the East and gold from *Ophir.* They were also instrumental in providing King Solomon with the cedar from Lebanon, which was used in the building of that glorious temple in Jerusalem. Of course, Herod had built another one after that was destroyed. It was a symbiotic relationship that was guarded with distaste and bred in suspicion! One could not exist without the other! It was a relationship out of necessity.

And finally, strike five! She was a woman, an unclean Gentile woman! She was not a daughter of *Avram* the chosen, or a descendent of *Yacov,* the blessed of YHWH. She was a woman whose lineage was doubtful and who could not enter the land that was given by YHWH Himself. Where was her husband? Could it be that she was a widow who had lost her husband and was clinging on to the only family she had, a child that was demon possessed and sick and dying?

She was a composite of what this world was! A hopeless pariah that was destitute, forgotten, and desperate!

She had no hope! She had heard that in the hills a day's journey from her house, there was a Miracle Worker who was healing people and casting out demons! News travels fast in these parts of the world! How could she even request healing from this Miracle Worker that she had heard about who was roaming the hills of Galilee? She did not know how He looked or where He dwelt. She was not permitted to enter the land of the Jews because she was a heathen and as such, unclean! She was worse than a dog! Unless. . .Unless. . .He just happened to show up in her tiny little village hidden in the mountains. How likely was that to happen? The odds were not in her favor, and her daughter was terribly sick, demon possessed, and tormented! Only a mother's heart knows the pain and the suffering of the child of her bosom. It was she who had carried this child for nine long months in her womb. It was she who had brought her into this world. It was from her breasts that the tiny little child had suckled! She was there when she took her first steps. It was just like a mother to notice the sickness first. How tragic! *The pain from a mother's heart only God can understand.*

When you are totally devoid of all hope and when frustration, destruction, worry, and sickness confine you and eat away at your very soul and you have nowhere to run to and no one to turn to, it is then that the Master comes in search of you. How many times in these miracles we have seen this *modus operandi* of Heaven's Creator God? When we lay bleeding and wounded and forgotten by the wayside, it is He who bathes our wounded and dying souls. It is He who steps into our realm of confusion and hopeless despair. It is He who sweeps us into His bosom and places a canopy of grace over us and whispers, *"Fear Not! For I am with you! Be not afraid! For I am Your God! I will heal you and uphold you! I will build your broken walls and heal your infirmities. . ."* Hallelujah!

She had way too many strikes going against her.

"He is here! He is here! The Miracle Worker from Galilee is in our town!" She could barely believe her ears! Could it be? Is that even possible! Her search had ended, and her journey of faith had just begun!

She hounded Him! She found Him! He was trapped in her tiny little world with crumbling walls and broken doors. He had entered her nightmare, and she would not let Him just walk away. Ah, the persistence of a mother's faith on behalf of her daughter. She would not take no for an answer. She could not afford to miss this one chance in a lifetime. She would hound Him and find Him and would not let him go unless a miracle happened.

She found Him reclining in a home feeding on some dry bread, full of crumbs! If only she had blessings the size of the dried up crumbs that the dogs were feeding on. The chosen can have the meal; let me just feed from the crumbs, the bits and pieces that even the dogs bypassed!

She was asking for crumbs from the table. She was not asking for a gourmet meal and a sumptuous feast. Just a few crumbs from a table that was lavished in plenty to feed a *"kunarion"* (a puppy dog).

How much does it take to feed a puppy! Not a whole lot! And puppies are good at doing one thing. They will howl and whine until they have food and their bellies are full. And then they will fall asleep, oblivious to their surroundings, until the next meal. They are unlike the big ferocious dogs that can be disciplined and trained to eat only at certain times. Puppies know only how to complain, and they can! They are sort of like newborn babies. When their stomachs are full, their whole world is at peace!

The Master is so tender with her. He calls her a *kunarion, a puppy dog!* He had come in search of this Canaanite puppy dog that was howling in a darkened world with no one to feed her or give her the crumbs of blessings. Her world was dark! Her daughter was sick! Her life was at the crossroads of despair and hopelessness! We have lost something in the translation. Jesus' tender words reach out to her as He says, *"It is not right or is it appropriate to take the bread that is given to children and feed it to puppy dogs!"*

Wow! Without even a second thought she shoots her answer right back at the Master, full of innuendos! Her words slice through the very heart of God Himself, and for once He is speechless *"Even the puppy dogs eat the fallen crumbs!" suggesting that unless you make my belly full, I will be howling and whining and carrying on! You will get no rest until I am fed! Are you ready for my whines? You might be the great Miracle Worker, but I will hound you until I get a resolution for my sick little girl! And I haven't even started yet! Are You ready to be hounded by the desperate cries of a mother standing in the gap for her daughter who was sick? Never come between a woman and her child! You will help her, and I will not let you go!*

Oh if we could have the faith and the persistence that she showed for her sick girl. It is sort of like Jacob wrestling with the Angel of God all night long and saying at daybreak, *"Unless you bless me I will not let you go!"*

There was nothing hidden about her. She was transparent! He came looking for her, and He was in her neighborhood, and she would not let him go unless her sick girl was made well. *She will hound him, exploit Him, beg Him, argue with Him, plead with Him, twist His words, and shoot them right back at Him and in the end get what she came for. The healing of her daughter! She would not take "No!" for an answer. You can call her an unclean Gentile, and you can abuse her, accost her and even call her a dog. But she was on a Mission! She was a mother interceding for her sick child!* No wonder Jesus responds, *"For saying this, your daughter has been made well!"*

He came to His own! His own rejected Him. But she, a heathen, sought him until her belly was full with His crumbs. She hounded Him until she herself was satisfied! She sought Him until her daughter was made well! If only the world had come after Jesus the way this *heathen Canaanite, Greek, Syrophoenician Gentile woman had.*

I want to leave you with this one thought! She had five strikes against her! She was miles away from the Master! She was stuck in a village in the mountains! *But when He entered her world,* there was no way she was going to let go of him. He was *trapped* in her world! The tables were turned! The hunted became the hunter! And Jesus responds to that persistent faith! *"But as many as received Him, to them He gave powers to become the children of God."* Even to howling, whining, hungry puppy dogs!

As this story winds down in a remote mountain village over-looking the city of Tyre and the shimmering turquoise waters of the blue Mediterranean Sea, the Gentile woman fades into the pages of the Synoptics, and the Master goes in search of another hungry puppy dog howling in the dark Galilean night!

16
Three Days

ημεραι τρεις

Jesus called his disciples to him and said, "I have compassion for these people; they have already been with me three days and have nothing to eat. I do not want to send them away hungry, or they may collapse on the way."
Matt 15:32 (NIV)

Great multitudes of people followed the Master all the time. They were lame, blind, maim, deaf, dumb, sick, men, women, children, zealots, rebels and outcasts of the society—they all followed Him. Some followed for a healing and others for entertainment, and many had hidden secret motives!

The people who were well stayed back and worked in the villages as carpenters working with olive wood, or as fishermen fishing in the Sea of Tiberius, or as bakers baking bread, or as shepherds in the fields, or as farmers cultivating the land, or as common laborers digging wells or breaking rocks for roads, or as blacksmiths sharpening the swords of the Romans. The rest of the people were useless for the Jewish economy!

It seemed that there were way too many sick people! If you lived to be forty years old, you were doing pretty good! They had no sewer, no running water, and no physicians to treat the poor of the society! Only the influential and the wealthy sick could afford the price commanded by physicians. These so-called *"physicians"* extorted great amounts of money for their healing potions, and most of the times, their potions did not work. Those who were sick and poor just waited for death to knock

> He was their only hope in a world that was crushed beyond repair and cursed beyond hope. Death and dying were the normal course of the events of the day! *What hope did they have?* None.

at their door! So, when Jesus burst on the scene, he obviously attracted the poor who are sick! These people hung on to his every word and hoped for miracles at every turn, and He never disappointed them!

Three days without food!

Well, if you are fat and plump and well fed, after two days the body will compensate for the lack of food by consuming the fat and the muscles! Three days of "fasting" is actually good for people who are well-fed. But when you are skinny, sick, lame, and maim, you are starting off with a handicap and you don't need to lose any more weight. This was the condition of the group of people who followed Jesus! They could *not afford* to go on starving! Their bodies were already *starving* when they started following Jesus! Three days without food, they could become delirious and might even die.

Sick and hungry and weak and faint! You get the picture! They were a multitude of people who would witness some great miracles in their lives! They were thirsty and hungry and in need of a Savior! They followed Jesus. He was their only hope in a world that was crushed beyond repair and cursed beyond hope. Death and dying were the normal course of the events of the day! *What hope did they have?* None. They were no strangers to a world filled with sickness and hunger and pain! *Theirs was a life doomed for death and damned for the fires of hell.* They were cursed by God and marked for suffering for the sins they and their generations had committed as purported by the clean-cut rabbis with their gold and pure wool *tallit* (prayer shawls) in their rabbinic discourses each Shabbat!

They were the people who were hopelessly entangled in a web of punishment. *They were made to believe that they were pawns in the hands of an Eternal Being who disliked them.* They were sinners in the hands of a God who would destroy them in this world and torture them in hell's flames in the world to come! The rabbis made sure that they understood that their sickness was a direct result of their sins!

What a miserable life! In this hopeless world of sickness, He came! He was a breath of fresh air in this pungent and stagnant cesspool. *The Creator God Himself walked among His contorted, dwarfed, and sick creation that was afflicted and marred by thousands of years of sin and corruption!* This day His heart was filled with compassion! Here was God Himself and His creative heart was filled with a deep sense of concern for the maimed and the downtrodden. He was capable of loving every one of them. He could see into the lives of each of them and feel their pain and suffering like no one else could! Here was God reaching out into their miserable present. No wonder He was full of compassion!

Three days with no food, and they were famished.

So, Jesus tells the disciples, *"Let's get them something to eat!"*

Not only does He feed them with spiritual food and heal their diseases, now he wants to take care of their very specific need of hunger!

But Master, we have a big problem! One problem! With a capital "P!" Where can we find bread to feed all these people! All we have are seven pieces of bread and some shriveled up dried fish! This seems to be the standard! There are people. . .people are hungry. . .there is some bread and fish. . .they never run out of fish and bread! A beggar's lunch! But that would suffice! Just give the Master something, anything, and He will provide and take care of you! So the miracle is repeated!

Heaven hears the praise of the Creator! "Baruch atah Adonai, Eloheynu melech ha-olam ha motzi lechem min ha-aretz" (Blessed are You God, King of the Universe, who brings forth bread from the earth.). The prayer for the bread reaches the throne-room of the Father Himself. Does God ever *not* answer the prayer of the Son? Never! A selfless prayer, not for Him but for these unclean children of His creation. He had to feed them. But He would not do it unless it was authorized and blessed by the Father Himself. What a Holy and perfect example! Complete harmony! The Trinity swoops into action, and the hillside becomes yet another witness to the glorious interaction of God in a hopeless world. The lame are made well. The blind receive their sight. The demons are expelled, the deaf hear, the dumb speak, and the hungry are fed. What a wonderful Savior! The bread is multiplied and so is the fish! The people are satisfied, physically, mentally, and spiritually!

What can we say but bow down in utter amazement and worship the God who chose to enter a realm infested with disharmony and save a wretched and a miserable soul like me! Hallelujah!

May I leave you with one thought? That day in the desert when faced by Satan and harassed by demons, He had gone without food for forty days, not three days! He was hungry, tired, thirsty, and lonely! He could have made stones into bread, and He could have satisfied His hunger! No one, not even the angels, would have questioned Him! But He wouldn't! Too much was at stake! Today, all stops are opened! The hillside above Capernaum explodes as unseen angels dance in unity, demons flee in terror, and the fallen sons of God praise Him for the miraculous works that they are witnessing. That day, a little bit of heaven burst on the grassy slopes of a hill covered with bread, fish, and dancing sons of God! Could it be that Heaven touched Earth that day?

17

"My Only Son"

μονογενης

A man in the crowd called out, "Teacher, I beg you to look at my son, for he is my only child. A spirit seizes him and he suddenly screams; it throws him into convulsions so that he foams at the mouth. It scarcely ever leaves him and is destroying him. I begged your disciples to drive it out, but they could not."
Luke 9:38–40 (NIV)

Matthew's account: *Have Mercy! He is an epileptic. He falls into fire and water!*

Luke's account: *Teacher I beg you! Heal My Only Son.*

Mark's account: *Have compassion, help us. . ."Help my unbelief!" He cried with tears! Jesus speaks to the demons, "I command you. . .come out of him. Enter him no more!"*

The composite picture we get from these accounts is rather a painful one. The father's only son was sick from childhood! The child's mind was distorted! His brain was destroyed. His speech was convoluted. Satan had taken possession of his precious little son. No one could heal him, not even the disciples! *"Lord, have compassion on us. Help my unbelief and heal my boy, my only boy! I know only You can! I beg You!"* It is the cry of a father pleading for the life of

100

his only son! Such is the cry of every father pleading for the life of his son! That cry reaches the ear of the Creator as He commands, *"I command you demons of hell. . .come out of him. Enter him no more!"*

Three accounts each adding a little more to the desperate plea and the hopeless situation that is presented in this incident. A com-

I did the right thing! I brought my son to your disciples. I did not want to bother you. I begged them to heal him. They could not. Now I am coming to You! Can You? Could You? Will You?

posite picture made with tiny mosaics of pain and frustration stare at us with unblinking eyes. *Words are thrown around in sincerity. We in turn gently and carefully pick up these painful words of a father and examine them! These are pearls in the ocean and diamonds in the sands of Namibia!*

We pick them up and hold them against the Sun. The rays ever so gently shed an extra hue of purple or a touch of deep blue to the cry of the father! His words are like uncut gems. Shimmering rays of colors explode from the voice of this frustrated father pleading for the life of his only son! Could they shed a little more light into this story of frustration?

Let us plunge into this desperate story of a father's frustration.

Luke has the father "begging" Jesus for a healing. The man could have *asked* Jesus for a favor. He could have *demanded (Greek: aitew)* that his son be healed. He could have *explained (Greek: zeitew)* to Jesus how he had searched and spent all his life savings seeking a remedy for this ailment! He could have come up with a litany of exclusive words to *request* a healing from Jesus. But he uses a simple word. He *begs (Greek: deomai) Jesus,* which implies an urgent need, a desperate call from a father on behalf of his only son, the heir apparent who was demon possessed! It paints a picture of a beggar waiting outside the walls of Jerusalem begging the passerby for a morsel of food!

Luke would use this same word in two of the miracle stories of Jesus that he recounts. The leper and the Gadarene demoniac both *"beg"* Jesus. The leper *"begs"* Jesus for a healing, and the demoniac *"begs"* Jesus not to torment him! Luke also tells us that the Father had previously *"begged"* the disciples to heal the boy, and they could not! Now in frustration he climbs up the ladder and *"begs"* Jesus!

Could He cast out the demons that were trying to destroy his son, even though His disciples could not? The implications are huge. It is a subtle but a strong accusation that points its bony and quivering finger at Jesus and tells Him that *His* disciples had no power and faith and know-how in releasing this boy from demon possession! There is even a tinge of accusation that Jesus probably did not *train* these disciples adequately, and as such, the failure to heal this boy rests squarely on the shoulders of Jesus' inability to equip the disciples properly to deal with demonic activities. The man is *begging* Jesus, but he does not let the disciples off the hook. He tells Jesus that he is frustrated because he thought that the disciples could take care of the problem, but they could not! His faith is wavering, and he is just about to throw in the towel and give up. So he reaches out to Jesus! *I did the right thing! I brought my son to your disciples. I did not want to bother you. I begged them to heal him. They could not. Now I am coming to You! Can You? Could You? Will You?* You can only sense the level of frustration as he falls at the feet of Jesus and begs like the leper and cries like the demoniac, *"Lord I beg You. . .Do not torture me anymore. . .I am living in this hell each day, ever since the birth of this boy. . .Please heal my son."*

The cry does not go unnoticed by the Master!

Only Luke mentions that this boy was the *"only son"* of this father! What are the implications here? As the only son in a Jewish family, you are the heir apparent to all the wealth, traditions, and the prayers that are said every day. As the only son it was your duty to follow in the lineage of *Avram. This man's lineage was at stake!* Could it be that as this father states his case in front of *the "only begotten Son,"* Jesus looks at the man and sees His own story there? No one could set Jesus free! The Father God would walk the hall-ways of Caiaphas and Annas and watch His own son being slapped upon and spat upon, and He would cringe as a crown of thorns was pressed on that forehead. He would be at the cross as His Son, *His Only Son* would cry out in agony, *"Eloi! Eloi! Lama sabachthani!"*

God the Father would be at the cross with silent tears as He watched His own Son being tormented and taunted by the demons of hell. He would hear the words *"It is finished!"* escaping the bleeding and the parched lips of that Word that became flesh and willingly died to prove to the Universe that His father was just and kind and loving! He would watch as water and blood poured out as a Roman spear pierced the side of *His Only Son*. He would be at that garden tomb, as demons and satanic forces surround the place of burial and dance around in victory! He would be at that empty tomb on that resurrection day when the greatest miracle of all times would set *His only begotten Son* free from the clutches of death, and man would have access to eternity! All that the Father God could do was watch *His only begotten Son!* He could not intervene! If He intervened, salvation would be forever placed on hold! Satan would be just, and heaven would coil back in defeat. God could only watch *His only begotten Son* pay the price for sin!

But for now, an earthly father begs the Divine Creator for the life of *his* only son! *Jesus would enter that realm of spiritual warfare!*

Mathew's account is very simple! He pleads for *"mercy"* and he uses a very interesting term regarding the sickness of the boy. The boy was *"selayneazomai."* He was *"struck by the moon,"* and thus a lunatic; by implication the boy was crazy. Incidentally, it will be only Mathew, the tax collector who makes a medical assumption that this boy is in need of psychiatric counseling and deliverance! Saying that a person is *"demon possessed"* is far less easy to comprehend than saying that the person is crazy! At least we have known that Jesus can cast away demons! But to restore a person who is *out of his mind?* That can only be done and orchestrated by the Creator God Himself who created that mind! There was something that was wrong about this boy! He was defective! He was born with a few of his marbles missing! He was handicapped, and as such, demon possessed! Only God could cure Him. He was born with a defective brain, and only God can re-create him!

Matthew uses this term *"selayneazomai"* to be struck by the moon twice in his writings. Both these usages involve crazy people seeking out a cure only God could provide. He mentions that they were even bringing in people who were *"moon struck"* from as far as Syria! God in action! Healing even the crazy ones! Restoration takes a new twist in the gospel of Matthew! This tax collector had witnessed crazy people before, and this was nothing new to him!

Matthew has the father of this *"crazy-moonstruck"* son pleading for *mercy! Mercy* seems to be the theme in Matthew's rendition of the miracle stories. He sets the stage by having Jesus declare, "Blessed are the *merciful. . ."* in the Beatitudes. And then he has the two blind men crying to Jesus for *mercy*. He has the Canaanite women pleading for *mercy*. He has this father once again begging for *mercy*. The two blind men outside Jericho demanding *mercy*. And he closes his argument for *mercy* by accusing the Pharisees and the scribes for not showing *mercy! Mercy! As the prophet Isaias writes, "In His love and His MERCY, He redeemed them. . ." Mercy! The depth of that word only God can understand. The heart of Jesus is moved with mercy, and He responds in His mercy! What a merciful Savior, one who forgets our past in mercy and steps into our distorted present in mercy and takes us to the home He has prepared for us, in mercy!*

Oh infinite and incomprehensible mercy!

Mercy responds to the cry of an earthly Father, takes on a human form, and steps into the arena of demons and the powers of hell!

In Mark's rendition of this story, a unique perspective is presented. Mark portrays the father pleading with Jesus and asking Jesus to *strengthen his unbelief!* How can we or anyone blame the father as he pleads with Jesus, *"Lord! Help my unbelief!" He was frustrated and crushed beyond any hope! He had tried everything under the sun to cure this boy, and finally he brings the boy to Jesus! Jesus was not there, but His disciples were, and they could NOT heal him, and now Jesus arrives at the scene. "Oh Divine Master, Creator of Heaven and Earth, grant me faith to believe in the impossible." He cries with a barely audible voice as tears roll down on a well-marked course on his cheeks! Such was the faith of the father! The boy was crazy, and the father was losing his mind! And the demons were rejoicing.*

It is time for a showdown. Mark would present this encounter with surgical precision. Jesus looks at the boy and with words that can send chilling fear into the heart of the author of fear itself, commands, *"I command you. . .come out of him. And enter him no more!" Wow! The command has been given. Satan, from now on you have NO jurisdiction over the life of this boy! He has been redeemed and ransomed, purchased and paid for, bought and marked for eternity by the Creator God Himself! You will enter him no more! Never again will you have the freedom to torment and torture this family! No more!* The command was given while the boy was still *"moonstruck"* and crazy. That is how powerful the words of the Master are! They can reach beyond our defective brains and cure that which is broken, distorted, and empty!

When you cannot think for yourself and someone takes hold of the Master on your behalf, praying an intercessory intervention on your behalf, the Master responds to that prayer of faith, and commands are given. Salvation is unleashed, and all heaven rushes to implement heaven's directive!

Demons disappear, and the boy is made well! What a journey! What a story! And the Master commands, *"Enter him no more!"* Hallelujah!

Let me leave you with a simple thought. He was crazy! He was lost in the domains of the evil one. His mind was wasted. He lay bruised, bleeding, all alone in the camp of the enemy. He could not think for himself. It took a father's persistent faith to pray on his son's behalf. Jesus enters the scene and the rest is history!

Where are you today? Do you know of someone that is "moon struck" and crazy and out of his mind? Have you approached Jesus with your requests on his behalf? It is time for you to seek Him out and cry out, "Heal him Lord! But help my unbelief!" Hallelujah! Heaven rushes to answer your prayer, your simple prayer on someone's behalf!

That day, a father rejoiced and heaven watched as God restored an "only begotten son" and gave him back to his interceding father!

That day in Palestine, Mercy marched in where demons had nested and destroyed the forces of hell and redeemed fallen mankind!

18
The First Fish

πρωτον ιχθυν

". . .go to the lake and throw out your line. Take the first fish you catch; open its mouth and you will find a four-drachma coin. Take it and give it to them for my tax and yours."
Matt 17:27 (NIV)

Only a tax collector would remember a miracle involving tax. It is a comical event! But this is one of the miracles that Jesus performed! It is also one of the most dangerous discourses that Jesus was engaged in! It was okay to heal a blind man or cause the lame to walk or chase away the demons of hell. These were religious matters involving religious laws of the Jews! But to speak in favor or against taxes would get you killed. You did not want to incur the wrath of the Romans! All ears were attentive to the discourse on taxes as those that collected the temple tax pursued Jesus with a question!

Rome existed on taxes! When Rome was a powerful country, they conquered people and looted their land. That in turn strengthened the financial status of Rome. Money poured in from defeated lands. However, Emperor Augustus, in 27 AD, decreed the "Pax Romana," the Roman Peace. Simply stated, Rome would no longer engage in military conquests, but would exist in a state of peace with all its neighbors. While in theory it sounded magnificent, it created a problem. Since Rome was not conquering people and places, its coffers were now devoid of any money! To solve this bankruptcy, Rome taxed its people, especially those who had been conquered. Therefore, taxation was the means

> Go and catch a fish that will be waiting for you! A fish waiting with a coin in its mouth! *Almost laughable!* God does have a sense of humor!

of survival for Rome's existence. To speak against taxation meant that you were speaking against the Caesar himself. That meant rebellion, and that would earn you death on the Roman cross!

There were three kinds of fish that were found in the Sea of Galilee. *Sardines* were the most common fish, and the sunny little village of Magdala, tucked away by the shores of the sea of Tiberius, specialized in pickling these sardines. It was a poor man's fish and was well received among the local people. The second kind was the *biny fish*. These were the most expensive fish and were used in banquets and weddings by the rich people. This fish supplied the Romans. The third kind of fish found in the Sea of Galilee was the *musht* fish. This was the tastiest of the whole lot. These fish carried the fertilized eggs in their mouth until they hatched! These fish were intelligent! They protected their young in their mouth! Once the baby fish had grown to size, the parent fish picked up shiny objects in its mouth to "scare" the baby fish that had grown bigger and were now seeking refuge in the apparently too-small mouth of the parent fish! Thus it was common to find in the mouth of the *musht* fish shiny objects such as a coin or colorful stones and pebbles. However, one cannot predict which fish carried what in their mouth. That only God would know, and here is where the miracle lies!

During the time of Christ, you paid two taxes! It was the law that any Jewish man who turned twenty was taxed with a temple tax, two *drachmas* per person. The civil tax was collected by the Romans in *denarius!* But the Romans collected both these taxes. The concept of the temple tax dates back to the days of Nehemiah. Note: *"Also we made ordinances for us, to charge ourselves yearly with the third part of a shekel for the service of the house of our God." Neh 10:32.*

The temple tax was initiated with Moses. Note: *"This they shall give, every one that passeth among them that are numbered, half a shekel after the shekel of the sanctuary: (a shekel is twenty gerahs) an half shekel shall be the offering of the LORD. Every one that passeth among them that are numbered, from twenty years old and above, shall give an offering unto the LORD." Ex 30:13–14.*

There was a constant ongoing debate among the poor and the learned whether any form of tax should be collected. That was a very touchy discussion. The poor stated that the Temple tax was limited to the time of Moses and Nehemiah! The priests emphasized the fact that the words of the Torah are eternal and that the temple tax extended throughout all generations. The Romans, in turn, agreed with the priests since they skimmed off a certain portion of the temple tax for themselves. How you answered the question of taxes could make you extremely unpopular! If a Roman soldier heard that there was a Jew who was not paying taxes and was advising his listeners to do the same, that would be reason enough for crucifixion, since that would be cause for a rebellion! If, on the other hand, the people heard from Rabbi Jesus that they should pay these taxes, Jesus would become the end point of some Jewish Zealot's dagger!

Jesus was being baited. He was being watched by the spies among the Jews, the Romans, and the Zealots! The Master skillfully answers the question. *"The kings do not tax their children, do they? But let us not entice anyone to sin* (Greek: *"skandalisomen"* from which we get the word *"scandal"*). *Peter, you go to the sea of Tiberius, catch the first fish that you find. Open its mouth and you will find a "stater" coin which would be the temple tax for two people. You and me!"*

The *stater* was worth two *didrachmas*. The *stater* was circulated by the Greeks 800 years before Christ, and the people were aware of its value and usage! The *stater* was not an unknown coin. It was this popular and expensive coin that would be inside the mouth of a fish! What are the odds of that? I cannot help but wonder if those who baited Jesus with the question went with Peter to see if what the Master said was a reality! Would the first fish that they caught have a *stater* coin in its mouth? I wonder if Peter felt the pressure as he cast the baited hook into the shimmering blue waters of the sea of Tiberius, half expecting, half hoping!

The miracle was not that the fish contained the coin in its mouth. That would be too simple of an explanation. Jesus could have asked Peter to keep on fishing all day until he found that right fish with that right change. Or He could have asked Peter to turn the rock over and find some *drachma* that had escaped the purse of a traveler on his way to Babylon! None of that happens in the miracle story! Go and catch a fish that will be waiting for you! A fish waiting with a coin! *Almost laughable!* God does have a sense of humor!

The miracle was couched in three basic "fish" facts. *Fact 1. There were fish in that sea of Tiberius that collected shiny objects. Fact 2. That fish had to have collected the exact expensive coin, a stater! Which it did! Fact 3. The fish had to be at the right place and moment in time!* Which it was. *The miracle was the fish!* The Creator God who created fish on the fifth day, according to the Genesis narrative, once again creates a fish that would carry the exact money, at the exact time and place and orders that fish to wait for the exact person to come by! It was a very simple miracle. But it was a powerful miracle. It was a poignant miracle that answered the tax question posed by the priests. Only Matthew would narrate this story. A simple question was asked! *Should we pay temple taxes?* Instead of a simple *"yes" or a "no,"* Jesus causes a miracle!

I want to leave you with one thought! A seventy-foot *whale* was waiting for Jonah at the right time and the right place. A tiny little sixteen inch long *musht* fish was waiting with a coin in its mouth for Peter, at the right time and the right place, and it was the first fish! What are the odds of any of these? Only God could orchestrate something like that! Period! Only God! I wonder if Peter took the fish home to his family or if he dropped it back into the sea!

I would have dropped the miracle fish back into the Sea of Tiberius. This was one fish I would not have cooked!

19
Jericho

ιεριχω

*Then they came to Jericho. As Jesus and his disciples, together
with a large crowd, were leaving the city, a blind man, Bartimaeus
(which means "son of Timaeus"), was sitting by the roadside
begging. When he heard that it was Jesus of Nazareth, he began to
shout, "Jesus, Son of David, have mercy on me!"*
Mark 10:46–47 (NIV)

Jericho! This was the oldest city in the world. This city existed
thousands of years before Moses and Joshua. This was the city in
which *Rahab* the harlot hid the Hebrew spies. This was also the final
city in which *Elisha and Elijah* would be together, until that day
Elijah went up to heaven in a chariot of fire! It was also the city out
of which *Zacchaeus the* wealthy tax-collector would emerge with a
new conversion and a changed life. This is also the destination of the
story of the *Good Samaritan,* and this is the city where *bar-Timaeus,*
the blind beggar, begged day in and day out, even on the Shabbat!

I don't even have a name. The people called me *bar-Timaeus,*
son of Timaeus. I have no family, no friends, not even a dog that I
could call my own. A beggar was cursed of the gods. And a blind
beggar was doubly cursed of the gods. I am just a heap of dust slowly

melting into the dirt that covers my brown and dirty cloak, my only possession on this earth. I did have a few prized "belongings!" A crooked stick to steady me as I walked and a plate to catch the kindness of the passersby! I don't recall when it was that I had taken a bath or had a full square meal! I just ate what fell on my beggar's plate. I am a dying glob of dust that was waiting to return to the dust out of which the gods created me! *I was a nobody! Until that day. . .*

> *I knew that this man who called the dead from the grave would fulfill my only desire that haunted the dust heap of my mind! I pointed again to those empty sunken sockets that had never housed an eye and I said, "Rabboni, I want to see!"*

It gets hot in Jericho! Dry heat, mercilessly beating on my uncovered head! This was the city known for the hardy *Sesban* plant that grew in abundance. Great for goats and sheep as fodder, these hardy shrubs provided the cool shade that my body needed so bad! Dust! Dust and choking dust! Even the *Ain of Alisha* (the spring of Elisha) was nothing but a trickle. Mind you, the city is hot because it is in the same depression where the salt sea is located, and that is hot! Hot! Hot! This is the city that overlooked the *Sea of the Waters of Death!* I have heard the rabbis arguing about King David's flight from Absalom and Zedekiah's flight from the Babylonians through this *Wadi Qilt*, which connected Jerusalem to Jericho! But then what do I know? I am blind!

I sit by the ancient crumbling walls in my own filth day after day begging from these people who would make that *"Ascent of Adumim,"* an eight-hour fifteen-mile walk from Jerusalem to Jericho! This was a tough city. Thieves and would-be thieves frequented the city. No respectable Jew would be caught in this city that boasted the best dates in the neighborhood!

It was the famous Passover week! One week from now would be *The Passover!* Those hypocrites celebrated the day when the angel of death destroyed those that didn't have the lamb's blood on the door post! *Just some ancient folk tale!* I had never been inside a synagogue anyway! I never understood any of that. No, sir! Never been beyond the walls of this filthy town. *Wish I could go to Jerusalem. Wish I could see the Temple! Wish I could see the palaces of the great kings! Wish I could see my face! Wish I could see the smile on a child's face! Wish I could see what I ate! Wish I could see!*

The Passover meant that there would be lots of visitors, and that would mean that I would be well fed! I had to stake my claims and map out my "zone" very carefully. I had the prime spot, right beside the gate that led into Jericho. I had claimed that spot years ago and had fought to maintain that prime piece of land. You see, there were hundreds of beggars who sat around the walls surrounding the city of Jericho. Each of us had a designated spot that we claimed and clung to. You move into a place belonging to another beggar, you are a dead man! We guarded this dry and dusty dirt heap with our own lives!

We were not wanted *inside* the city, but *outside* the city was fair game! No beggars were ever allowed inside the city. They would stone us if we were seen inside the city! We were "unclean"...well, that is an understatement! Of course we were unclean. Who would want a filthy, dirty blind beggar bumping into clean Jewish rabbis in the market place or sitting beside them in the synagogues. *Come on! Are you crazy?* We were all cursed outside the walls, and here we would stay, and one day we would die, and our bodies would be dragged to the dirt pile that was not too far from where we begged! It would be food for the dogs and the vultures! Nobody would touch us or be kind to us! *We were the living dead!* We knew our place in this world!

It was a hot and dusty day, just like any other day! I have been sitting there for what seemed like hours. I had heard that there was a prophet in town! They called Him *ben-Yosef.* They said that He had healed many people. He had even raised some people who were dead! If He could do that, then He might be the promised *Messias, the Son of David!* Well, who cares! *He is probably sitting in some rabbi's house drinking some cool wine from Galilee and being sumptuously fed and feasting on goat cheese, dates, and some delicious kosher meat and pickled olives!* He would have no time to *heal* me! Who would even notice me? I am one of the thousands of beggars forgotten along these walls. Even IF, *even IF* He just happened to come outside the city, how would I know? *I have never heard His Voice.* I have never touched His garment. I have never seen His Face, and for that matter, I have never seen *my face!* I know of no one who would lead me to that *Prophet!* It is a hopeless wishful thinking in the real sense of the word! There is no way I can meet this man. Unless, of course He recognized me! How would He recognize me? He doesn't even know I exist! Let me stop daydreaming and focus on the present job at hand. I need to clank my plate a little harder and shout a little louder, *"Alms for a poor blind beggar! Alms for a poor blind beggar!"*

"Make way! Make way!" someone was shouting.

"What is happening?" I asked. I did not want to be run over by a mob of angry people or a hoard of Roman soldiers or a caravan of camels from Babylon headed into the city!

"It is the prophet, ben-Yosef the Nazarene; he is coming this way!" the beggar beside me replied!

What? The prophet is headed my way! I had one chance of a life time. I do not know how far He was from me. He could be near or far! All I know was that he was coming my way. One chance in a life time. I would seize this moment! I shouted with a voice that even surprised me! "Son of David! Ben-Yosef! Have mercy on me!" Did I just say that? Well, not loud enough. I shouted again and again. "Son of David! Have mercy on me!" Louder and louder till I was hoarse. I will not quit until He heard me! I could hear someone say, "Be quiet! You beggar!" Ha! This was my moment! No one would step into my moment in history! No one would tell me to be quiet! The more they told me to shut up, the louder I cried! "Son of David! Have mercy on me!" I shrieked and yelled and screamed at the top of my voice, clanging and beating on my beggar's bowl!

Then something strange happened! "A pair of rough hands seized me and a voice spoke, "Come here, the prophet wants to speak to you." Me? He heard me? He wants to speak to me? A nobody, a dust heap, a living dying waste of human filth? He heard me!

I threw aside my cloak I struggled to my feet with the help of my stick and leaped up. The hands dragged me to the prophet!

113

A voice spoke, "What do you want?" Years of anguish and pent up emotion welled up in my soul! With hands shaking with excitement and uncertainty and expectation I pointed to the empty sockets in my eye. Those sockets that had housed a thousand flies and were now festered with sores! I knew that this man who called the dead from the grave would fulfill my only desire that haunted the dust heap of my mind! I pointed again to those empty sunken sockets that had never housed an eye and I said, "Rabboni, I want to see!"

This is the only thing I had ever wanted. I wanted to see! If He only knew the desire of my heart! This is all I wanted! I wanted to see the trees, the sunshine, people's faces, the food that I ate, children laughing and Rabbi's arguing, camels, goats, water, my own face...

"Go, your faith has made you well". . Just like that my eyes were opened and I could see colors and dust and people and animals and sunshine and camels! No fanfare. . .no drum rolls! I was blind one second and the next instant, I could see! The first face I saw was the face of this Son of David, this ben-Yosef! It was a ruddy brown bearded face looking at me with a smile.

It was. . .It was. . .It was the face of God!.

I would witness some strange things as I followed him to Jerusalem and beyond. It would take me a lifetime to learn about Him! My Rabboni, ben-Yosef, The Son of David, The Son of God, The Messiah!

Let me leave you with this one thought! Bartimaeus was blind. Jesus gave Him sight. Matthew says *". . .and he (Bartimaeus) followed him!" Bartimaeus followed Jesus! Could it be that Bartimaeus followed Jesus during that last week of His ministry on this earth? Jesus would be crucified in one week and He was on His way to Jerusalem from Jericho. This was the last blind man that Jesus would heal before the crucifixion. Did Bartimaeus follow Jesus to Bethany and then on to Jerusalem and to Calvary? Was he at that triumphal entry shouting at the top of his voice, "Hosannah! To the King of the Jews! I was blind but now I see". . .Was he watching Jesus in the garden of Gethsemane, with those eyes that were once blind? Was he following Jesus in all those five trials, as He was hustled from Annas to Caiaphas to the Sanhedrin to Pilate to Herod and back to Pilate? Was he melting in the shadows of the Passover week as an observer of the final events leading to the crucifixion of Jesus? Was he one of those whose voice was drowned as he yelled with tears rolling down those eyes that were blind just a week ago "Do NOT crucify Him, He gave me eyes to see!". . .Was he in the shadows witnessing these strange events and wished he had never received the gift of sight to observe the crucifixion of God? Could it be that the one who was blind was one of the last eye witness to all these events! Could it be that to the one who was blind, was shown Calvary, the Cross and an Empty Tomb?*

Could it be? I was once was blind, but now I see! If I were Bartimaeus, I would have followed this Man who gave me sight, all the way to Calvary and beyond!

I would have wept in agony at the cross and would have asked God to take away my eyesight!

20
The Fig Tree
Συκην

The next day as they were leaving Bethany, Jesus was hungry. 13 Seeing in the distance a fig tree in leaf, he went to find out if it had any fruit. When he reached it, he found nothing but leaves, because it was not the season for figs. 14 Then he said to the tree, "May no one ever eat fruit from you again." And his disciples heard him say it.
Mark 11:13–22 (NIV)

They can grow as large as 30 feet in height and their roots can go as far deep as 400 feet in search of water. They need a lot of sunshine to produce the fruit. Their large leaves provide a much needed shade in dry Israel. Ancient Egyptians and Greeks revered the fruit of the fig tree for its aphrodisiac properties! The juice from the leaves was used as an insect repellant. The *Torah* mentions that the Promised Land would be filled with olive oil, honey, barley, pomegranates and *figs!*

Why would Jesus curse a fig tree? What is the real meaning behind this *miracle?* All the miracles we have seen so far are positive ones. Every miracle, with the exception of this one, has shown the healing powers of the Creator God! They all have shown that God restores things. He does not destroy things, especially *fig trees!* Here

116

comes one miracle that does not fit the personality of a kind and a benevolent and a compassionate *Christos!* I can understand the concept of healing and casting away demons and calming the sea! But to curse a fig tree? Come on! Are you kidding me? This miracle makes no sense! Should all the *"miracles"* make sense? Was this *really* a miracle? Should this even be termed as a *"miracle"?* The cursing of the fig tree does not fit

This beautiful city along with its temple would be no more! The tree had refused to produce fruits! *The tree showed beautiful green leaves! But no fruits!* The tree would be fit only for fire! *Jesus wept!*

into the nice cubby hole that we have carved out called *"miracles."*

This miracle is sandwiched between two important events in the Passion Week. The first is the Triumphal Entry, and the other is the cleansing of the temple. In between these two episodes is nestled the cursing of the fig tree. *But why?*

King-Jesus rides into town as the physical King, openly declaring that He is the *Promised Deliverer.* The people are excited and seize the day and shout in unison, waving palm branches, *"Hosanna to the King!"* They are excited! They thought that here was their King who would overthrow the reign of the Romans and restore Israel to Solomon's glory days.

That day Jesus rides into Jerusalem as a king, as the Son of David. The people feel that the moment foretold by the prophets is now here, and there will be relief from the tyranny of the Roman Empire. They would rise up from the ashes again, and Israel would revert back to the glory days of David and Solomon! *There is nothing that can stop this now.* The twelve disciples are excited beyond a shadow of doubt. They are invincible. *The matter is settled. Jesus has been declared King by the people!* I wish the story ended there! It doesn't.

How did Jesus feel about all this excitement?

Jesus wept! He wept over Jerusalem and her constant refusal to listen to the prophets. He wept because He saw the destruction of that city in a few years. He wept as He saw their rejection of Him, the Source of their destiny. He wept as He saw the time of the end!

She was the holy city. She looked beautiful and perfect now, basking in the glory of that magnificent temple that shown like burnished copper in the morning sun. He wept as he saw the present rejection and the future destruction! As their *"King"* He would see beyond the present day celebration and witness the destruction of the city of Jerusalem. Sorrow and anguish flood through His compassionate heart as He sees this sheep scattered in the hills being butchered by the forces of Rome! *He wept! God wept!*

He saw the Jewish Zealots wage a losing war against Roman *General Titus*. Titus would starve Jerusalem! The siege would start on a Passover day and would last hundred and forty-three days. Titus would destroy over a *million inhabitants* with his well-armed and stockpiled thirty thousand Roman mercenaries who were even now getting ready for one of the most spectacular destruction of Jerusalem ever to be recorded in history. The glory of Israel, the beautiful temple that housed the Ark of the Covenant would be sacked, burned, and razed to the ground! Titus and his army would mercilessly destroy this city, and the Jewish nation would be annihilated! The second Diaspora would begin. *All because this tree with all these verdant and green foliage, full of show and celebrations and rituals had refused time and again to produce fruit!* Over and over, she that was supposed to have provided food for the weary and to have given light to the Gentiles and be an example to the heathen nations had become barren, *fruitless!* The tree was full of beautiful green leaves, but there was not a single fruit! How sad! *How tragic!* She would become worthless! She would compromise, wheel and deal, cause people to stumble, cheat, lie and prostitute! She would wander so far away from God that when He appeared, she would crucify Him! *The green beautiful tree had no fruits!* It had become barren! *Jesus wept!*

The God-Jesus marches into the marble and gold temple that Herod had built with meticulous precision and care and cleanses it of all filth and impurity. He openly declares that He is God in action! He was not pleased with their filthy acts of cheating and thievery within the very halls of this place of worship! He would not and could not condone it! The Jehovah God of the Old Testament would cleanse this beautiful edifice. This magnificent temple would be leveled to the ground by Titus, who would become the next Caesar. On April AD 70, Titus would post his invincible elite *Tenth legion* under the banner of the *Mighty Roman Eagle* on the Mount of Olives directly in line with the Temple. One hundred and forty-three days and almost four-and-a-half months later, in August, he would torch the temple and burn it to the ground and take all its possessions as a victor's spoil to Rome, just as Nebuchadnezzar had done six hundred years ago! No more temple! No more sacrifices! No more outer court, inner court, holy place, or the Most Holy Place. No more temple artifacts! No more altar! No more laver to purify them. No more table of shewbread or the golden menorah. No more altar of incense or the Ark of the Covenant! No more finely carved and pricey artifacts that now graced this marble and gold dwelling of YHWH. *"The slaughter within was even more dreadful than the spectacle from without. Men and women, old and young, insurgents and priests, those who fought and those who entreated for mercy, were hewn down in indiscriminate carnage. The number of slain exceeded that of the slayers. The legionaries had to clamber over the heaps of dead to carry on the work of extermination."*[1] This beautiful city along with its temple would be no more! The tree had refused to produce fruits! *The tree showed beautiful green leaves! But no fruits!* The tree would be fit only for fire! *Jesus wept!*

The Man-Jesus seeks to satisfy His hunger. The fig tree was a symbol of Israel. They could not even acknowledge Him as one of them! They were plotting to murder Him. The people would reject Him as their King. The priests would reject Him as their God. Even His disciples would reject Him as the God-Man! *He searched for a single fruit in that tree; there was none.* Not a single one! Not one who would truly and honestly be with Him all the way through Calvary's cross! They would ALL *en masse* desert Him, flee from Him, curse him, and betray Him! No one understood Him. They all, even Peter, even John, would run away from Him. And Judas would sell him for a few pieces of silver. And in a smoky alley, warming his hands over a Roman fire, Peter, the burley, outspoken fisherman, would curse his Friend who was being arrayed in a makeshift courthouse in the second watch of the night! There was no fruit, not

---

[1] Milman, The History of the Jews. Book 16. Crebermuda. *Retrieved 2013–08–31.*

one! *Not even a single rotten fruit from last year's crop was present on that tree. Not even this tree, this physically green and healthy looking tree had any fruit! Jesus wept!*

Symbolically Jesus performs one of the most frustrating *"miracles,"* if you want to call it that, and sets a reminder for those who would frequent the winding road from Jerusalem to Bethany that Passover week and the weeks following and shake their heads as they saw a withered fig tree on the way to Herod's glorious temple!

The Creator God does something that is out of the ordinary. He becomes the destroyer! It must have hurt the Son of God as He Himself curses this lusciously green tree! Wow! Heaven shrinks with surprise. Demons flee in confusion! *The Universe witnesses one of the strange acts of God!*

The fig tree withers, and in a few days Jerusalem would crucify the Creator God! And Titus would annihilate Jerusalem and Herod's priceless temple! Nothing would make sense!

Not a single, fruit; what a tragedy!

Jesus wept!

21

"Be Quiet!"

φιμωθητι

🌿

Just then a man in their synagogue who was possessed by an
impure spirit cried out, "What do you want with us, Jesus of
Nazareth? Have you come to destroy us? I know who you are
—the Holy One of God!"
Mark 1:23–24 (NIV)

*H*e stumbles towards the Synagogue on the Sabbath! The only
place a demon-possessed man should be, in the place where
God was, where the Torah was, where loving people were!

The Gospel of Mark should have been called the Gospel of
Peter. Tradition has it that young Mark was writing these stories
and encounters of Jesus that were told to him by the elderly fisherman, Peter.

Mark has eighteen miracles being performed by Jesus in this
shortest of the four gospels. Jesus is portrayed as the Son of God,
The Beloved Son, the Holy One of God, and the One who will baptize His people with the Holy Spirit, all in the first chapter. It is quite
remarkable and impressive!

Yet it is in this Gospel, that young Mark would portray Jesus not
as a mighty king, or an interceding High Priest but as the humble

His conscience screams at him. The voices in his head remind him of all the sins that he had committed. The last place he should be was in the presence of God! The giants of hell refuse let go of another soul seeking the Creator God. He would have to make this journey to the feet of Jesus all by himself. . .

servant who, even though was the *"agion tou Theou"* (the Holy One of God), would make Himself a *"doulos"* (a servant, a slave) who would serve His People!

There are seven Sabbath miracles, and two are mentioned by Mark in the first chapter. Let us plunge into one of the stories and see it for ourselves.

Jesus was baptized in the Jordan and was tempted in the desert by the demons. He calls His disciples, and the first thing He does is to go to the synagogue on the Sabbath. That in itself is a story, isn't it? He goes to the one place on earth that housed all the people who had come to worship. He needed their presence to strengthen him. He needed to bask in the presence of those who had gathered to worship the Father. He needed their acceptance, their love, and their faith as He embarked on this dangerous mission to save a lost world!

The Sabbath was the highlight of the Jewish society. All week long you slugged and slaved and barely existed. However, the *Shabbat* was a time when families got together from sunset Friday to sunset Saturday and worshiped the YHWH God who had with authority and clarity given them the *Torah* and the Commandments. The Fourth Commandment etched in stone on Mt. Sinai said, *"Zakor ha yom Shabbat!"* (Remember the Sabbath Day).

The *Shabbat* was a time to be in the synagogue. Here you met with your friends and discussed the Torah and prayed and sang and rejoiced. It was a time to mend the brokenness you experienced during the week. Everyone gathered on the *Shabbat* at the synagogue.

Here at the synagogue, He is confronted, challenged, and acknowledged by the demons. Incidentally, you did not do any work on the day. If you were found *"working"* on the Sabbath, you would be thrown out of the synagogue, or worse, you could even be killed.

There were strict laws around the observance of the Sabbath that had evolved that were constantly enforced! What you could not do and should not do on the Sabbath Day, the Day of the Lord, *"Yom Shabbat"*, was imparted with punitive actions by the temple guards and the synagogue leaders!

The man was obviously sick. But, he was not sick enough to be nonfunctional or morbid. He did not need the assistance of someone to bring him to see Jesus. He came on his own free will. There was a small ember of *"Godness"* still glowing in the dark and eclipsed world in which he lived. The ember would recognize the eternal fire that was present in Jesus. *The man would recognize through the cobwebs that choked his conscience and see the pure and Holy One of God in front of him.* With utter hopefulness he would reach out to this Man who was the only one who could release him from the clutches of the demons of hell that are tormenting him!

All he can do is walk towards the synagogue. He would go to the synagogue as a last resort. He would seek out God!

He had no family to bring him to Jesus. There is no mother to intercede on his behalf; nor is there a father who would plead for this man's deliverance; neither does this man have any friends who would take him to the Master. *He has nobody.* No one that could guide him as he sought God! He comes to Jesus just as he is!

This is the pathos of this miracle!

Just as I am, possessed and tormented by the demons and wishing release, I come to You!

He stumbles in the bright noon daylight and reaches the door of the synagogue. The reading was almost over, and Jesus had just finished the *Shabbat* service. Would the demons allow this man to reach the Savior? Would they release him just enough to reach the Savior in time? A battle had begun. The captain of the army of the heavens was just a few feet away. The host and armies of hell cling on to this man. He is bound with invisible chains that no one sees, and none but he feels the effect of those silent compromises that he had made in the dark. None but he knows the secret deals that he had made in the recesses of his mind that now hold him bound, gagged, and chained to the forces of the demons. His conscience screams at him. The voices in his head remind him of all the sins that he had committed. The last place he should be was in the presence of God! The giants of hell refuse to let go of another soul seeking the Creator God. He would have to make this journey to the foot of Jesus *all by Himself*, just like one day Jesus Himself would have to make that journey among the jeering demons of hell to the hill of the skull. This man would crawl with one last ounce of strength left in him and seek out the captain of heaven's armies.

Jesus knew exactly where this man was. He was there when he was knit in the secret places and birthed in some Galilean hut on a dark and cold Palestinian night. He knew this nameless man's darkest sins. He knew the exact moment when he started on the downward path of self-destruction and silent compromises. He knew the nature of this man's sins. It was He who at one time had held him as the apple of His eye. The Holy Spirit had pleaded with him. The Holy Spirit had pleaded a hundred times with him and had lost all the battles! But there was still a glimmer of hope. One last chance. *He stumbles on to the stage in the synagogue. Heaven watches with pregnant expectation for the showdown at the synagogue as demons of hell scream at God!*

God faces fallen man and the confrontation begins, not in a desolate desert but in the house of God!

What follows next is a dialogue between the *El Shaddai* and the *fallen angels!* He knew them too! He knew every one of these demons that are within this man. He had created them perfect once, but they had been deceived and had chosen the dark side. The war was on. He rebukes the demons, and they in turn scream and cower in front of the Almighty YHWH!

The arguments and the pleadings of the demonic angels are cut short with one command! *"Phimotheiti"* "Be muzzled!" Wow! *The powers of darkness cannot fight against the commands of El Shaddai!*

Jesus uses this word twice in Mark. He would today tell the demons to be *"muzzled."* And in a few chapters, He would once again tell the storm in the Sea of Galilee to be *"muzzled."* It is the same word. Only He who created these angels once upon a time before war broke out in heaven and Lucifer was defeated and cast to this earth and took with him a third of the angels, had the authority and the power to *"muzzle"* these fallen angels. No wonder these demons recognized the commander of the armies of heaven and shrieked in fear and dread *"I know who you are, THE HOLY ONE OF GOD!" What a fearful testimony! That alone should send chills up and down anyone's spine! They recognized heaven's Son. They once served Him. They had once walked with Him and communed with Him. They knew Him! They could not stand in the presence of the One who had defeated them in heaven. They could not be in the presence of the Great I-AM! The demons flee in terror at the sight of the glorious Creator God. Jesus is seen in heaven's fullness as the captain of the armies of God and not as a humble peasant!*

The man is made well, just like that! One minute filled with demons, and the next He is sitting at the feet of Jesus! He who dwelt in darkness now sees light. He sits in the synagogue sobbing at the feet of the Creator God! And Jesus moves on to set another captive free.

Let me leave you with this one thought. *The man came to Jesus on the Sabbath! He came to church on the Sabbath. He was demon possessed, and he came to church! He came to the only place where he knew (troubled and crazy and demon possessed as he was), he would find God. Jesus went against what was considered the norm on the Sabbath day! Jesus pierced the laws that were set by the Jewish leaders and "broke" the Sabbath by setting a man free from the clutches of demons! Jesus restored this man on the Sabbath. According to the laws of the Jews, Jesus worked on the Sabbath! For all intent and purposes, Jesus broke the Sabbath observance to a million pieces. He would do it a total of seven times. He would heal chronic diseases that need not be healed on the Sabbath. He would chase away demons that could have "waited" for another day! That lame man at the pool of Bethesda could have been placed on hold for one more day! The crippled woman, the man with dropsy, the man with a withered hand sitting in the synagogue, Peter's sick mother-in-law—all these sick people could have waited for one more day! They could have been "cured" on a Sunday, or a Monday, or a Tuesday!*

Why did Jesus so blatantly break the Sabbath laws? A simple answer is that God was in Christ reconciling Man. It did not matter what day the miracle took place! Should we follow in the footsteps of the Master? Should we be restoring lost souls on the Sabbath? Have we become calloused and insensitive on the Sabbath? Has our desire for Sabbath observance overtaken the tears that God sheds for humanity on the Shabbat, the Queen of all days? Does God the Father "rest" on the Sabbath as He sees millions of His creation lost, hungry, sick, dying, and wasting away on the Holy Shabbat? Forgive me Father! How could God "rest" when humanity is crying and dialing 911, and the whole world is burning in the flames of hell? Any day is redemption day, even the Sabbath! Especially the Shabbat! Hallelujah! Thank God, Jesus never rests!

(Note: Jesus would perform seven very poignant miracles on the Shabbat! And this would infuriate the rabbis so much so that they plotted to get rid of Him. How sad!

He would heal a lame man by the pool of Bethesda John 5:1–18;
He would drive out an evil spirit Mark 1:21–28;
He would heal Peter's mother-in-law Mark 1:29–31;
He would heal a man with a withered hand Luke 6:6;
He would heal a blind man John 9:1–16;
A crippled woman would walk again! Luke 13:10–17;
A man with dropsy would live to see another day! Luke 14:1–6)

22

"Be Opened"

εφφαθα

Then Jesus left the vicinity of Tyre and went through Sidon, down to the Sea of Galilee and into the region of the Decapolis. There some people brought to him a man who was deaf and could hardly talk, and they begged Jesus to place his hand on him.
Mark 7:31–32 (NIV)

Only Mark records this miracle that takes place in the region of *Decapolis,* the ten cities. In fact, two times Mark records Jesus entering the region of the *Decapolis,* and both those times Jesus would engage Himself in spiritual warfare! He would wage an open war in the tombs and the dwelling places of the demons and win every time. This miracle is no exception!

Deca means ten; *Polis* means cities. The dreaded ten cities of the heathen dotted the eastern region of the Jordan. The Jordan River was unlike the mighty Nile of Egypt or the Tigris and Euphrates of the Babylonians. It was just a trickle of water that connected the Sea of Galilee to the Sea of Death. However, this river served as the boundary between the land of the children of Ammon and Moab and the children of Judah.

His command reached out like a flash of lightening on a dark and stormy Galilean night into the recesses of this soul that was chained to a silent world and broke those chains into a million pieces and set this man free from years of torture!

This river is the lifeline of Israel! On the western side were Jerusalem, Bethany, Nazareth, and Mt. Olives with green farm land and luscious orchards of fruit and olives, and the shimmering blue waters of the Mediterranean Sea. But on the eastern region of the Jordan were the ten cities that stretched from *Damascus* in the north to *Philadelphia* in the south. With the exception of *Scythopolis*, all the cities of the *Decapolis* were located in the dry desert region stretching into *Nabatea,* the dead, dry desert inhabited by camels and sand and dark foreboding mountains! What a contrast: one side the turquoise *Mediterranean* and the other side the dry desert of *Arabah, the wilderness.*

No, we did not consider those cities as the *"Promised Land!"* We did not want them. The despicable Greeks and Romans inhabited these lands along with the untouchable Samaritans! These heathens worshiped *Zeus* and prayed to the Roman Emperors! This was in contrast to the One God who we worshipped! They clearly broke the laws of the Torah! You see, after the death of Alexander the Great, the generals of his army decided to live in these regions, and they built fortress cities. These cities became powerful centers of Greek culture and conflicted with our own Jewish traditions and our way of life, a way of life prescribed by YHWH. No way would a respectable Jew be caught in these cities. These cities were the nesting grounds of demons! *Their worship, culture, foods, holidays, philosophy, and way of life in general was diametrically opposed to our traditions!* And only this trickle of water divided us from the nest of demons! We did not trust these hordes that raped our women and cheated us in business transactions! Let them be doomed and banished to the fires of hell and may the curse of the Almighty be their constant companion! Every time Jesus traveled here, we hugged our daggers closer to our tunics. One had to be careful in this region, especially a Jew!

We were within the region of the *Decapolis*. There was a sick man who was deaf and mute and demon possessed! We had seen this *modus operandi* many times. The closest friends or family members brought the sick people to Jesus, and He would heal them. They would beg him on their knees and cry out to him to heal their loved ones. The picture was the same everywhere! At times I wonder where the Master got all that energy to do this over and over again. Never once did He say any harsh words to those that brought the sick to Him. At times He wouldn't even ask for an explanation. He would just look at the sick ones, and with a command, a touch, a glance, a movement of the hands, He would heal their diseases and cast out the harassing demons.

They *begged* Him. The Greek word is *parakalousin*. It is the same root that is used in describing the Holy Spirit, the *Paraclete*. This word *Paraclete* is translated as *"advocate," "intercessor," "teacher, "helper"* and *"comforter."* Picture this: these heathens were doing the work of the Holy Spirit on behalf of this man! Doesn't that just warm your heart? They were *"advocating"* Jesus on behalf of this man, just as the Holy Spirit would *"advocate"* on behalf of us in the heavenly courts after Jesus leaves this earth and the *Paraclete* descended on Pentecost!

There were two sets of people who begged *(parakalousin)* Jesus in the region of the Decapolis. One set of people begged Jesus to leave their region when they found out that He had not only healed the demoniac, but He had sent the demons into a herd of pigs and the demons had cast the pigs into the sea of Tiberius. This group *begged, or advocated* Jesus to leave their town. The second group of people brought a young man to Jesus and *begged* Him to heal him! This group of people interceded on behalf of their friend. They wanted a healing. They respected Jesus! Both these groups of people were from the region of Decapolis, a region that was populated by Greeks, Romans, and unclean Gentiles!

Jesus responds to their request! I have never seen Him do this any other time. I still don't understand why He did what He did! He does three strange things!

1. Jesus *isolated* this dumb and mute man. He gently took hold of this man's hands and took him away from the crowds into the privacy of His presence. *Just Him and the young man.* Isn't that so much like the Master? He never embarrassed you. He kept you private, and not once did He expose your sins to the whole world. Look at what He did to that prostitute who was brought for stoning! She should have been stoned. She was guilty. Everyone knew that, and she was caught red handed. *But* He knelt beside her and ever so gently started scribbling on the dirt the private sins of her accusers! He had all the right to expose the sins of those pious, rock totting hypocrites. He could have blazed the sky with their sins and embarrassed them! But He didn't! He protected them just as He protected the prostitute! Even in my own life, I would learn that He would deal with me as if I mattered. But that is a different story!

2. We watched Him as He put His fingers in the man's ears and touched the man's tongue with *His saliva.*

3. Jesus then *groaned* as though in some pain and looked up into the heavens and said one word, just one word in Aramaic, *"Ephphatha!" (Be opened!) There were no arguments, explanation, talking to demons, nothing, just one word: "Ephphatha!" a barely audible groan of a whisper! You know what happened? His command reached out like a flash of lightening on a dark and stormy Galilean night into the recesses of this soul that was chained to a silent world and broke those chains into a million pieces and set this man free from years of torture! Instant miraculous healing. Just one word. Nothing else! The sick man spoke! He heard! That man who was deaf and mute began to speak and hear! "Ephphatha!"*

I wish now, looking back at all these miracles, I, Peter, could have understood this Man Jesus, this *ben-Yosef!* Was He God? A prophet? An angel? The *Messias?* Who was this man that could multiply food, cast out demons, heal the leper, the lame, the blind, the deaf, the mute, and tell the storm to *"be muzzled"* and command a deaf ear to *"be opened!"* and even call the dead to *"come forth"* from the grave! My head is spinning as I try to wrap my simple fisherman's logic and try to explain these extraordinary events to young Mark!

I, Peter, would live to see more than just a few more miracles. *But for now, today, in the Decapolis another deaf man heard and another dumb man spoke! Because someone interceded on behalf of this wretched soul, advocated on his behalf and begged Jesus for a healing. They became like the Holy Spirit to a mute and a deaf man and brought him to Jesus and thus procured comfort and healing for a soul lost in a dark and a lonely world. A nameless group of people became a "Paraclete!" They took the place of the Holy Spirit!*

Let me leave you with this one thought! The miracle was not just the healing of this young man. Yes, this was quite a powerful incident! It is not every day that the dumb spoke and the deaf heard! To me the miracle was in the fact that these people who lived in the Decapolis, knew beyond a shadow of doubt that Jesus could heal their deaf and mute friend. They took on the job of the Holy Spirit! Even the heathen in the region of Decapolis, believed in the miraculous powers of Jesus. It was so sad to see that my own group of close friends who followed Jesus did not possess even a fraction of the faith that this despicable people of Decapolis had in Jesus! We would hear Greeks, Syrophoenician Gentiles, heathen Roman centurions, and even demons confess that this ben-Yosef was God's Beloved Son! But when it became our turn, we would run away and desert and curse him!

Could it be that I have become so used to having Jesus around that I had forgotten who He really is!

Have I become too comfortable and have I missed out on the persona of the real Jesus?

As I pondered the events of the day, in the distance I could hear a rooster crowing!

My chance would come only too soon on a dark Friday in the courtyard of a high priest! Would I become a "Paraclete" for ben-Yosef?

131

23
Ripple in the Waters!

ταραχθη το υδωρ

*"Sir," the invalid replied, "I have no one to help me
into the pool when the water is stirred.
John 5:7 (NIV)*

*T**he stench is unbearable!* All the invalid cursed by Elohim, sick,
maim, deaf, mute, rotten dying rejects of human society with
bleeding and ulcerated extremities gathered here around this pool!
The pool was murky and putrid and smelled like sewers during hot
summer days when water was scarce! They came from all over the
world to the heart of the city of David, waiting for a miracle year
after painful disappointing year! They waited with dying hope! Most
of them had already given up. Their expectancy had turned to self-
pity, anger, frustration, and abject surrender to the inevitable fact
that they would die one day here, only to be replaced by yet another
hopeful who sought healing from these waters!

Beth-hesed!. . ."*A house of mercy*" or "*The house of graceful
waters.*" It was more like a *house of horrors!* The sick waited in
agony for the waters of the pool to be agitated. Tradition claimed that
an angel from *Elohim* came and stirred these waters, and the first one
who got in, was instantaneously healed! *Wow!* If only that were true!

But tradition and fable gave these sick ones hope to face another day; just maybe they could be next!

The waters used to purify the temple sacrifices joined the waters of the pool through some subterranean passage. During Passover, the blood of a thousand sacrifices would seep into the underground springs that fed this pool and colored the waters of this pool into a strange pinkish hue! So, tradition had it that YHWH Himself blessed these waters!

Only if this poor sick man had known that He was on God's shortlist! How was he to know that? He had sent silent cries and voiceless petitions in secret for thirty-eight years. He knew that none of these petitions had ever gone beyond the walls of this pool.

The pool had five porches. It was no small pool! It was 165 feet long and 320 feet wide! It was so old that even King Hezekiah and Isaiah the prophet mention it in their writings. It started as a small water reservoir and expanded through underground caves and became a huge, one acre complex that was divided into two sections with five porticos!

The pool was located just outside the sheep gate entrance to the temple. It was through this gate that the unclean shepherds brought the sacrificial sheep to the temple! From the unclean shepherds, the sacrificial lambs were bought for the temple and the unclean children of Ishmael provided the frankincense for the temple service! And the unclean Samaritans provided the grain that was needed for the bread in the Holy Place! They were all unclean! The shepherds, the beggars, the foreigners, and the Samaritans! And must we even mention King Herod, whose hands were soaked with the blood of a thousand murders, who financed the building of this great temple? The system was so convoluted! And the priests who gouged the people and manipulated the temple system were all unclean! Yet the wretched, quarantined to this one part of Jerusalem, hung on to the traditions of an angel and a ripple in the waters!

And they waited here. . .with hope. . .

What was Jesus doing here on the *"qodesh yom Shabbat?"* *(the Holy Sabbath day)*. Shouldn't Jesus have been in the synagogue? Shouldn't He have been arguing some fine point of theology with the rabbis on this *day, the queen of all days?* Shouldn't He have been resting on the Day of Rest? *No!* Not my Jesus. He was seeking souls, lost souls bound in despair and chained to physical and mental sickness! *A composite picture of humanity etched in the porches of this house of mercy was screaming to Him for mercy, and God could not keep silent and "rest." He would visit and heal on His Day, the Sabbath Day!*

Jesus *"saw"* him and he *"knew"* him. The all-seeing eye of *Elohim* scours this bedlam of sick souls gathered around this pool clinging to a fable that had long since disappeared into the pages of history! The eyes of mercy roamed the *"house of mercy"* and in compassion rested on this soul that was waiting for death to come knocking on his doorstep.

It is with divine accuracy that He chooses this soul, the most frustrated one among this deformed and degenerate filth of human sickness and waste. He brings out the checklist that He had made when He and His Father and the Holy Spirit had mapped out His days on this earth. It is a list that contained all the people who He would personally visit! Angels of light point to the man. *They are on a mission!* Only if this poor sick man had known that He was on God's shortlist! How was he to know that? He had sent silent cries and voiceless petitions in secret for thirty-eight years. He knew that none of these petitions had ever gone beyond the walls of this pool. How was he to know that God had a list of people who He had to personally visit while He was on this earth? *This weak and forgotten soul was one of them on heaven's short list!* He would not ascend up to Calvary without bringing hope to this weak and destroyed soul! The salvation of man would not be complete without the healing of this *son of Avram!*

He *sees* him, and in that instant He *knew* him. He knew the pain and frustration, rejection and trials that had beset this *son of Avram* His servant. He knew him as no one else would. God was reviewing his file! No! His file had already been reviewed! Wasn't it He who saw his plight long before he was even born? One page after another, one sin after another, one victory after another, one rejection after another had been reviewed, analyzed and had been forgiven. God was reconciling another lost soul! All that He saw was a dejected forlorn soul who had given up hope. His heart of compassion was filled with mercy, in the *"house of mercy."* God was at home! This is where He, Jesus belonged. This was His creation suffering. It was His creation that was lost and dejected in a cesspool of sin! It did not matter that this was the day of Rest! Heaven would teach earth the true meaning of the *Shabbat!*

This wretched and miserable soul had no hope, no one, no family, no friends, no wife, no church—*NO ONE to help him* as he watched the pool for thirty-eight long and frustrating years. *But no, not today.* He might have no one on this earth. But He had heaven's Son headed out to meet him and set him free. If only he could have known that!

Jesus *knew* him. Instant recognition. . .Jesus makes a bee-line for this soul lost in despair and self-pity. Heaven was reaching out to earth. *Demons flee in absolute terror.* A path of holy angels clear the way through this habitation of demons and accompany their Commander as He walks towards that man. Angels of light wield their swords of fire as they cut through this nest of demonic angels that have possessed this *"house of mercy."*

What a glorious picture when God meets man! What a powerful picture when the King of Kings and the Lord of Lords sets out to seek that which lay dying and wasting in the battlefield. *All stops are pulled. Heaven's Majesty on mission of Mercy on the Holy Sabbath Day, a Day when God meets Man!*

Jesus reaches this man. It is show time!

One question. One answer, three commands. Surgical precision!

Question: "Do you want to be made well?
Answer: "I have no one!"
Command: "Rise, take up your bed and walk!"

That's it. That is the extent of the whole conversation. He had lain sick for a life time of thirty-eight years! He does not answer the question posed to him by Jesus. And Jesus does not stop to discuss the answer given to Him by the sick man! All this man can do is look at his surroundings and his present state. I don't blame him. All that he has going for him is that ripple in the water, and he can't get to it in time! For thirty-eight years he had tried in vain, only to be disappointed time and time again! There was always someone ahead of him! He is just a bag of bones in a tent of loose skin! He feels sorry for himself, and he sees nothing, no one, not a single soul that could help him. For a brief moment he struggles with the question. *But Jesus bypasses his answer.* He does not even ask his opinion! He just gives him a three-part command!

He had to do three things. He had to rise up. He had to pick up the mat. He had to walk. *He had to obey! Not once but three times! The miracle could stop anytime if the man did not obey Jesus three times!* He did not even have a cane to prop him up! Three things he had not done in thirty-eight years. These three things would sap his energy unless he was infused from a source of energy that is greater than this disease! *"Rise, take up your bed and walk!" The commands resonate in the dark canyons of his forgotten mind! He has nothing to lose. . .*

In that instant, some hope stirs in that man's heart as he reaches out through the fog of thirty-eight years and looks at the face of the one silhouetted against the warm light of the noon day sun! What does he have to lose? He did not know who Jesus was. He had not even heard about Jesus. He had not followed Him. He had no family that was sitting by him to tell him who this Man who is talking to him was. He had not waited for the *Messias! He was an abandoned man sitting by a pool clutching to a long-forgotten fable and hoping for another day to dawn! He had no idea that heaven was watching this moment with pregnant silence. Would he respond?*

Nothing about this miracle makes sense! No one asked Jesus to heal this man, and this man did not ask Jesus for a miracle. All he did was respond to that one sentence with three commands *"Arise, take up the mat, and walk!"*

This nameless man who was lame for thirty-eight staggering years struggles to his feet, picks up his mat, and walks! Heaven cheers! Demons cower with hate!

Instant healing. Does the story end here, or is it the beginning of a new life?

There is a fourth command given to the man. Jesus finds him later in the temple and tells him, "Stop committing sins!" Wow! Arise, take up the mat, walk, and stop sinning! Only God could heal and only the Creator could demand!

Another one of those mysterious acts of God! Why didn't He heal the entire crowd? Why did He single out this man? We would never know the reasons!

However, let me leave you with this one thought.

Humanity is lying around the pool of mercy, just waiting and dying. Pictures of Darfur and Somalia, children with bloated stomachs and eyes filled with pus and flies haunt our minds. We see famine and people struggling to face another day! We just cannot handle this tragic picture. We flip to the next TV channel with the remote control as these faces cry out for mercy. We stare at a world gone crazy through the comforts of our own living room and leftover pizza! We look at our lives. We see our reflection in the mirror. Tragedy, pain, disease, divorce, loneliness, disappointments, rejection, and death glare through those red beady and tear-stained eyes of ours that have not slept in days.

We cry in desperation "Are You there? Do You even know I exist? Do You even care?" We are in Bethesda. We are Bethesda!

Somewhere in the heart of Orion's belt, God brings out the short list with my name on it. Heaven marches with its commander, as angels of light wield their swords of fire as they cut through this nest of demonic angels that have camped around my own life all these years.

There is a knock on the door, a ripple in the pool!

My name is on heaven's shortlist!

****

(Note: Jesus would perform seven very poignant miracles on the Shabbat! And this would infuriate the rabbis so much so that they plotted to get rid of Him. How sad!

He would heal a lame man by the pool of Bethesda John 5:1–18;
He would drive out an evil spirit Mark 1:21–28;
He would heal Peter's mother-in-law Mark 1:29–31;
He would heal a man with a withered hand Luke 6:6;
He would heal a blind man John 9:1–16;
A crippled woman would walk again! Luke 13:10–17;
A man with dropsy would live to see another day! Luke 14:1–6)

****

24

Ten Lepers

δεκα λεπροι

*Now on his way to Jerusalem, Jesus traveled along the border
between Samaria and Galilee. As he was going into a village, ten
men who had leprosy met him. They stood at a distance and called
out in a loud voice, "Jesus, Master, have pity on us!"*
Luke 17:11 (NIV)

A band of brothers, infested by the dreaded disease, roamed the
barren Samaritan wilderness, waiting for death to visit them.
    From Nazareth in the south of Galilee to Samaria was roughly
half way to Jerusalem. Forty miles south of Jerusalem is the southern
tip of the Dead Sea. Forty miles north would put you in Samaria.
Forty miles west would take you to the Mediterranean Sea coast,
and Forty miles east would move you into the dry hill country of the
dreaded Ammonites, the incestuous children of Lot!
    It was sixty-eight miles from Galilee to Jerusalem. Jesus, along
with his disciples, was traveling to Jerusalem. If they walked five
miles a day, this trip alone would take them almost two weeks. It
was quite the journey. Where did they stay? What did they eat?
Where did they rest? Who went with them? The Bible is silent on
these questions of survival. Moses had commanded that YHWH

I was hurting on the inside. I was dying! I was angry. I had no close family on the "outside." I had slowly settled into my lifestyle and was waiting for death. All that changed in a moment.

required every male Jew to travel to Jerusalem three times a year to *". . .appear before the Lord."* (Ex 34:23). Jesus would have followed the Law. And He would make the Passover trip, the feast of the Pentecost, when God gave *Moshe* the Ten Commandment on Mt. Sinai and the Festival of the Booths, which commemorated the wandering in the wilderness. He would have gone to Jerusalem during these three festival times — The Pentecost, The Festival of Booths and The Passover! Jesus traveled a lot. He walked a lot!

The picture of Jesus in a spotlessly white clean robe does not fit the Biblical or historical Jesus! He was more like a homeless transient living off the goodness and the kindness of the people who He came into contact with. I picture Him sleeping under the stars on warm nights, and I see Him in the early morning sitting beside the embers of a dying smoky fire, wrapping His dusty robe around Himself, warming His hands and poking the dying embers with an olive branch, talking to His Father. I see him taking shelter under an olive tree waiting for the storm to end. The picture of Jesus as *"one of us"* is hard to swallow.

As I grow older, that life that Jesus led seems more appealing to me! Jesus was hard and rough and rugged like the Samaritan hills but tender in heart like the poppies that dotted the Judean country-side in early spring. He was compassionate and kind, unlike a lot of us! But the story — rather, the miracle — today is not about Jesus. That would have to wait for another day. The story is about us! It is about a group of unwanted *"walking dead"* lepers who lived in the caves that dotted the dry and desolate hills in Samaria. These dry and rugged mountains housed caves in which dwelt the unwanted filth of the society!

The final leg of the journey from Samaria to Jerusalem involved the treacherous "Jericho Road." The road was dangerous and was called "The Bloody Road." A number of robbers and thieves and misfits hid along the mountains and lived in the caves and attacked the pilgrims who traveled with money to Jerusalem. It was a *cash highway* and the most popular road to take to go to Jerusalem. The pilgrims who headed to Jerusalem would have money and would carry only the best to sacrifice for YHWH!

We were the lepers, the outcasts and unwanted people who lived in Samaria in the north, far from the City of David. The *leper colony* as we liked to call ourselves dwelt in the caves around Galilee. We dare not step inside the confines of *"Jewish territory."* The Samaritans were unclean and were *not* recognized as people belonging to *Elohim YHWH!*

Our history is rather weird. Our ancestors were from Assyria and Babylon. We, however, intermarried with the Jews and claimed that we were "half" Jews. But the Jews in Jerusalem despised us and called us unclean. Well, that is an understatement! I was doubly unclean! I was a leper and a Samaritan! Twice cursed by the gods. Maybe the Jews were correct. Maybe I was unclean and the gods hated me!

I was not alone in the caves! We were a close-knit clan of ten lepers. This was our family. We would cry and laugh, eat and starve, and one day we would die together! When you are a leper, it did not matter what you were on the "outside." You were a leper on the outside and that is what the people saw. Who cares if you are a Jew, or a Roman or a Greek or a Samaritan? This disease was cursed by the gods. Neither *Zeus* nor *Apollo* nor *Elohim* liked us, and we in turn could not understand how the holy gods could curse mankind with this disease that deprived you of your loved ones and caused you to be despised and eventually kill you in loneliness, slowly! The ten of us had one thing in common. We were lepers who were rotting away slowly, and we were marching to death's drumbeat. God did not care about us! In fact, God did not exist! How could a Divine Being sit there and watch us suffer day after day like this? In resignation we waited for death to come our way! Little did I know what God had in mind!

I was hurting both physically and emotionally. It seemed that God had removed His face from me. I was a disgrace even in the society of lepers. I was hurting on the inside. I was dying! I was angry. I had no close family on the "outside." I had slowly settled into my lifestyle and was waiting for death. All that changed in a moment.

One day we had a visitor! That in itself was a rare miracle! But the message that he brought was even more fantastic.

He told us that in the hills of Judea there was a Miracle Worker who was healing people. He had healed the lame, the blind, the deaf, the mute. . .and one leper! *Did you say, leper?* Now he had my attention. We asked this man again and again if what he said was true. He swore upon *Elohim* that he was speaking the truth. He said that the name of the healer was Jesus, and he was from Nazareth; he was the son of *Yosef* the carpenter and he had a gang of twelve people who followed him everywhere! He never went alone anywhere! There was always a crowd that followed Him. I liked that! *He was sort of like us! Like the ten of us! We never went anywhere alone either!* I mused!

That story from the visitor held me captive for days. I would fantasize in the night time what I would do *if* that Miracle Worker came my way! *Would He even talk to me? Would I be able to recognize Him? Would He stop just long enough to see me? What if I was asleep when He came? What if I was on the wrong place at the wrong time?*

Watching for Jesus of Nazareth became my obsession! I would search the meandering dusty path and watch with bated breath day after day for a band of people! That visitor had left us with one clue. This *ben-Yosef* had a gang of twelve who followed him. *A group of twelve or thirteen! That was the key!* That shouldn't be too hard to notice. I would ask people when they came through our road, if they had seen Jesus! It was always the same answer, *"Get away you filthy unclean cursed Samaritan leper dog. Get away and stay away!"* Words lashed at me with hatred. I was beaten, chased out, spat upon! Despised. . .*God are you there?* Months slipped by. Nothing happened. My hopes were dashed on the rocks of despair. I slowly gave in to the reality that this Jesus would not be coming my way!

Each sunset nudged me a little closer to death. I knew I was dying. So was my family of lepers. It was the festival season. That meant only one thing. People would be traveling. Maybe. . .just maybe. . . .Once again my obsession resurfaced. I was on a hunt. *I was hunting for Jesus!* I was counting! Little did I know that He would be coming my way! I knew that if he was a Rabbi, He would have to pass through this road, which was the only road that connected Galilee to Jerusalem. I searched again. . . .Then one day I noticed a group of people coming down the dusty road. *1, 2, 3, 4, 5,* I counted *6,7,8,9,10,* I could barely contain my excitement *11,12,13.* . . .This is it.

I ran to the cave with excitement bursting from my hoarse and parched throat, scaring my half-dead friends. I shouted and woke up my family! *"Get up! Get up! Jesus is coming our way,"* I cried.

I pulled and pushed and dragged my leper family, and we approached the group of people with guarded optimism.

"Jesus, Master have pity on us!" I shouted.

I wanted collective healing.

A man who looked like one of us, dirty, tired, dusty, unshaven shouted back, *"Go show yourselves to the priests!"*

I could not believe my ears! He didn't touch us, ask us, or invite us. He just shouted back at us. Is that it? That was all I needed. I knew He could heal! I did not want an affirmation. The ten of us looked at each other stunned. Is this it? "Let us go to the priests!" We had nothing to lose and everything to gain. Off we went running. I could not believe what was happening as we walked the dusty road towards Nazareth. We were being healed! Inch by inch our putrefied bodies were being restored! We were healed. Just like that!

I could not let Jesus go without thanking Him. I turned back! I could see the gang of thirteen round the next bend in the road. I ran shouting and praising God. . ."Jesus. . .Jesus. . .Stop. Hallelujah. . .I am healed!" I shouted as I neared Him. He stopped, I fell down on my face, and thanked Him. A Samaritan leper cleansed from the inside and outside. . .I heard Him say to me,

"Rise, your faith has made you whole!"

Those words would haunt me all my life!

Let me leave you with one thought!

I was a leper, a Samaritan leper. I was unclean, unloved, despised, rejected, cursed, shunned, jeered at, kicked at, forgotten in some lonely cave in the hills of Samaria waiting for death to come

143

my way. I heard about Jesus. He became my obsession! I searched for Him. Then Life came my way! Jesus came my way. He cleansed me. He loved me, accepted me, forgave me, and snatched me from a leper family and grafted me into the family of God! He can do the same for you!

You see, I am one of the nameless disciples of Jesus.

No longer a leper, I am an heir to the throne of God!

Hallelujah! Thank you, Jesus!

****

25

Nain's Widow's Son

ναιν

Soon afterward, Jesus went to a town called Nain, and his disciples
and a large crowd went along with him. As he approached the
town gate, a dead person was being carried out—the only son of
his mother, and she was a widow.
Luke 7:11–12 (NIV)

S he was on her way to bury her only son in an unmarked grave!
"God sows." That's what *JEZREEL* means! The Valley of
Jezreel was sandwiched between Galilee in the north and Samaria in
the south. It was a fertile and green valley. Fruit trees and vineyards
dotted this valley, which was home to the village of Nain where the
next miracle takes place. The valley was located between Mount
Carmel in the west and the Jordan River in the east. This was the
valley in which the field of *Nabaoth,* was located. If you recall,
Queen Jezebel killed Nabaoth and gave the field to King Ahab.

This flat and beautiful valley became the staging point for some
spectacular and bloody wars between the invading armies of the
Egyptians, the Assyrians and the Babylonians. The valley also
boasted some great battles between the armies of Saul and the dreaded
Philistines. It was also around here that Gideon chose his 300 men,

> The procession meanders from her house, through the market place and the town square, and out the city gates. The lonely wail of a mother who has lost two men punctuates the valley with hopeless despair and haunting sorrow.

and destroyed the Midianites; Jehu's armies defeated the armies of the wicked Queen Jezebel here; and it was in this valley at Megiddo that Josiah was killed by the Egyptians. The valley was bathed in blood and soaked in treachery. *It might look green and luscious, but it was watered by the blood of ten thousand soldiers killed in a hundred brutal wars. It was here in this valley that long-forgotten heroes of great wars had lost their lives fighting nameless wars.*

From the village of Nain, you could see Elijah's Mt. Carmel in the west and the snowcapped peaks of Mt. Hermon in the north. The village was peaceful and set in an idyllic location, but its history was dark and penned in crimson blood!

She was a widow! She was also the mother of an only son. Having lost her husband she had no one other than her only son who could provide for her. Now he too had died! She was once again cursed by the *gods* and despised by the people in the village. Reasons for the death of the two men in her life were quietly whispered in the local markets and around the wells where the women went to draw water for the day. *"Cursed by God. . .committed sins in secret. . .her family must have been sinful. . .she killed them both. . .poisoned them. . .struck by the angel of death in their sleep. . .she caused the anger of Elohim to unfurl on her. . .attacked by Beelzebub. . ."* The list and silent accusations had no ending! She would bear the brunt of all the shameful gossip these Jewish women threw her way for the rest of her life! How could she survive the venomous attacks of those who once were her *"friends"*? How could she live among the people who boldly accuse her of being *"cursed by Elohim!"*

She was worse than a leper, condemned by the society and tormented by her peers!

Her whole world had come crashing on her. Laughter was replaced by sadness. Despair and hopelessness, rejection and gossip beat down upon her frail and grieving heart without mercy. Her joyful life was replaced by endless sorrow and utter despondency. *If only she could die and join her husband and her son,* then there would be peace in the battlefield of her heart. *She lived in Jezreel, her own personal Jezreel!* Now her son would join her husband among the tens of thousands that lay dead in the valley of Jezreel! She had lost the two most important people in her life. People who would have provided for her, cared for her, protected her, prayed for her and defended her. She was now vulnerable, an open book that could be ripped up, torn, shredded, and tossed into the fires of hell by those who had once been her friend and family. *Cursed by YHWH, she would roam the land of the living until one day she too would die of exhaustion and join her husband and her son who she was about to bury!*

With a heart that was heavy with sorrow and eyes that could shed no more tears, she gathers a few of the young men in the village to carry the lifeless body of her only son wrapped in a clean white linen and a makeshift open casket, to the burial grounds just outside the gates of the city in the Valley of Jezreel. A sad procession snakes its way through the city as hushed and painful whispers of her friends accuse her with words and looks that stab her every step of the way. The procession meanders from her house, through the market place and the town square, and out the city gates. The lonely wail of a mother who has lost two men punctuates the valley with hopeless despair and haunting sorrow!

A bend in the road reveals another group of people approaching the funeral procession. *The timing was perfect.* Headed by Jesus, the disciples and the large crowd draw near. Jesus sees the widow. Jesus hears her lonely cries. The heart of the Redeemer is once again filled with *compassion as God meets man in a funeral!*

God will meet man wherever and whenever an opportunity presents itself.

In the widow's eyes He sees the face of Mary, His own mother, who would one day wail at the *Hill of the Skull* for the loss of her Son and her husband. In that moment Jesus could not contain Himself any longer. The crowd comes to a halt as the Master commands, *"Woman, stop wailing!"* He approaches the coffin and touches it. *That which He could not do for His mother, He does to a total stranger!* Life from the Giver of Life infuses into the body of the dead young man as Jesus talks to the one who had been dead. *"Young man get up!"* The dead man is brought back to life. Jesus restores a broken life and wipes the tears of a widow!

The miracle is powerful but filled with pathos!

The heart of *His* own mother would be broken at the cross. For three days and three nights, until she heard from *Mary of Magdala,* the heart of that sweet mother at Calvary's cross that fateful Friday, would be broken, and there would be no one to wipe her tears, comfort her wailings and no one would tell her, *"Woman, stop crying!"*

It was Mary who was visited by the angel Gabriel. It was she who had housed Him in her womb for nine months as a young teenaged mother and had birthed him in a cave with sheep and cattle. It was she who heard the words of Elizabeth, Anna, the prophetess, and Simeon, the old prophet, at the temple. It was she who witnessed the shepherds, the Kings of the East, the star, and received the strange gifts from a distant land. It was she who had nursed Him and had taught Him his first steps, and had searched for Him for days at the temple. It was she who had kissed His first tears and held Him to her bosom and comforted His pain. It was she who had protected Him from harm's way as a lioness would, after the death of her beloved Joseph. It was she who had fed Him, clothed Him, washed Him, bathed Him, and taught Him the *Torah!* It was she who had singularly affirmed the fact that her Son was none other than the Great I AM. One day it would be her wail that would fill the *Hill of the Skull* outside the city of Jerusalem. Heaven would not comfort her, and angels would not appear to her bereaved soul. In solitude she would wail for three long days!

Jesus' heart was filled with compassion for this widow who was a total stranger. His heart must have been filled with grief as He saw in the mirror His own mother, who would go through what this nameless widow was now experiencing. Even His last prayer, " *Father, into Your Hands I commend My Spirit"* would be that which His precious mother had taught Him. No one would touch His coffin and raise her Son. What a tragedy! Three days in hell's darkest nights, the Son and the mother and all heaven would wait as demons of hell rejoiced over the death of God!

This is a miracle that is filled with deep emotions and sorrow and tugs at your heart!

Let me leave you with one thought!

Jesus' heart was filled with compassion as He saw this nameless widow mourn the loss of her only son. As I read and reread this miracle, the picture of Mary, Jesus' mother, grabs my own heart. *If only He could comfort His own mother from Calvary's cross.* The tears of that nameless widow of Nain were wiped by Him whose heart was filled with compassion. In a few more days there would be another widow, who would witness the brutal death of her only Son on a Roman cross. She would rend her garments, beat her chest, and wail heavenward as only a mother knew how, *"My God, My God, Why have you forsaken us?"*

That scream of agony and pain would pierce the thunder and lightning and the darkness at Calvary and would reach the gates of heaven itself to the empty throne room of the Father God. A knife would pierce her trembling and quivering heart as she witnessed her Son, her Only Son, bloodied and nailed to a cross, struggle for His last breath!

There would be no answer. Heaven would be silent! Angels would shield their own eyes. The sun would refuse to shine, and the graves would give up the dead! Darkness would cover the earth! The curtain in the temple would be rent! Demons would dance! God the Father would be in the shadows! There would be no one, none to comfort her grieving heart and bring her crucified and dead Son back to her. Three long and lonely days she would suffer the agony of death. The Father, the Son, the angels, and this earthly mother would spend three dark nights in hell.

O Mary, sweet mother of our Savior, *"Do not cry!"*

With tears in His eyes, Jesus sadly disappears from the pages of this story, raising the lifeless son of a nameless woman, as Mary, His own mother, not too far from here, prepares to replace the cries of the Widow of Nain!

26
The Royal Official's Son

βασιλικος

And there was a certain royal official whose son lay sick at Capernaum. When this man heard that Jesus had arrived in Galilee from Judea, he went to him and begged him to come and heal his son, who was close to death.
John 4:46,47 (NIV)

Herod Antipas, the son of Herod the Great surrounded himself with people he could trust. They were the royalty, the "Basilikos!" Herod was crafty, wicked, and conniving. After his father's death he became ruthless in governing Galilee. If he suspected anyone of sympathizing with the locals or being friendly with the Galileans, it was the end of them. He even divorced the beautiful princess of Nabatea, who he had married for political reasons, and stole the wife of his own brother and married her. Herod was power hungry. Nothing and nobody stood in front of him. In order to please Emperor Tiberius of Rome, he built the beautiful city of Tiberius on the turquoise shores of the Sea of Galilee. He made a number of friends and enemies. He had to maintain a good relationship with the Romans.

Galilee was not really a peaceful territory. It was far from Jerusalem and close to the rebellious Samaritans. It was the nesting ground for the dreaded zealots. If he could not keep peace, here, Rome would exile him and worse, they might get rid of him! He needed eyes and ears to maintain peace and provide him with a constant and a steady flow of news and information in this treacherous and unstable political climate. He demanded loyalty and allegiance. He gave those close to him special privileges and concessions. To this end Herod appointed numerous "Basilikos" who were given authority and power so that they remained loyal to him first and then to Rome. The "Basilikos" were a group of people to be feared! Their loyalty was to Herod!

He was not a blind beggar outside the walls of Jericho, or a demoniac guarding some empty tomb in the hills of Galilee, or a fisherman looking for a coin in the mouth of a fish, or a poor man in need of a free lunch! He had money, wealth and time! He was blessed by God and protected by Rome!

Herod Antipas would govern Galilee for forty-two years with a fist of iron and heart of steel. He would order the death of God on a Roman cross, and mesmerized by the sensual dance of a teen age girl, he would provide her the head of the Baptist on a silver platter!

This miracle centers around one of those who were the ears of Herod Antipas, the ruler of Galilee! A "Basilikos!"

Royalty! All the wealth in the world does not preclude you from sickness, disease, and death. However, if you are wealthy and money is not a problem, you could hire physicians who could heal that disease. And if you had connections, you might even get the physicians who served the community of the royalty!

All we know is that this man was of a royal lineage. He was not a blind beggar outside the walls of Jericho, or a demoniac guarding some empty tomb in the hills of Galilee, or a fisherman looking for a coin in the mouth of a fish, or a poor man in need of a free lunch!

He was a prominent person who was well connected; he had money, wealth and time! He was blessed by God and protected by Rome!

Being a son of the royalty meant a few things. The boy was used to an opulent lifestyle. He had everything: servants, fine clothes, respect, fear from the community, the choicest foods, and the best that life had to offer. If you were a *"Basilikos"* you were even entertained by the king himself! It would not have been uncommon for this child to have been taught by one of the finest teachers that Rome had to offer! You were a son, and that meant that you were the heir apparent to all the wealth of your family, and it also meant that you would carry the lineage of the family. So, the man was rich, blessed by the Gods, and in good favor with the aristocracy, but He was desperate; his son was dying! *What irony.* All the gold and silver could not buy health!

No one could cure the boy. None of the physicians could release his boy back from the clutches of this strange and horrific disease that had wrapped its deadly claws around this frail and weak boy! Potions, magical words and hidden recipes in some strange concoctions could not alter the disease of the *paidia* (the child).

It was twenty miles from Cana to Capernaum, two days' journey if you traveled on foot and less than a day on horseback! *The "Basilikos" determined that he would seek this Jewish Rabbi who had acquired the powers of healing! He set out with his entourage. You never traveled alone in Galilee!* He searched far and wide. He looked in every hut, asked at every market place and every synagogue, and checked with the local fishermen. *He was searching for Jesus!* The man lived in Capernaum, and I am sure that he would have heard about Jesus from the people there. In fact Jesus had turned water into wine at a wedding in Cana. You know how news can travel in weddings. That was the talk of the town. So when the man heard that Jesus was in Cana, and that He had returned to Judea, he went looking for him!

That was not a wise move. You see, the eyes of Herod were watching everybody. You could never trust anyone. If the news that one of the *"Basilikos"* of Herod went looking for Jesus reached the ears of Herod Antipas, this man and his family would be compromised and dealt with severely! Herod was already trying to get rid of John the Baptist for publicly accusing him of infidelity. And John the Baptist had placed his stamp of approval on Jesus of Nazareth. In fact he had called Him *"Lord!"* There was even a rumor being whispered by the Zealots, in the dark and smoky wine houses in Capernaum, that Jesus might very well be the *Messias* who would destroy the Romans, set the Jews free and restore Israel to the glory days of Solomon! That would mean, no Rome, no Herod, no *"Basilikos". Looking for a favor from the chief of the rebels was not a wise move. But desperation has no boundaries and love has no limits!*

There was no need to have *"looked"* for Jesus. He could have easily sent his people to *find* Jesus, and they could have arrested Jesus and brought Him to Capernaum. *But he took a chance! He took a chance of being misunderstood by Jesus, and being destroyed by Herod's spies!* The *"Basilikos"* traveled to Cana, a distance of twenty miles, searching for Jesus. He knew that if he could find Jesus, he personally would request, beg, and implore Him to accompany him to Capernaum and there Jesus would heal his precious little child! This was important to him! So with a retinue of bodyguards and supplies, he traveled to find Jesus. Sort of like Naaman who traveled to find Elijah the prophet! Or like the Kings of the East following a distant star! He searched for Jesus! His son was dying, and Herod would have to wait! He finally found Jesus traveling in the obscure, tiny, sleepy village of Cana, nestled in the plains of Galilee.

"Sir, come before my son dies!" This man who was loyal to Herod implored Jesus, to come to his house! Now that is an audacious request. The fears of treason were drowned in reality. It was a cry from the crushed heart of a father who was desperate. It would be the same cry that we would hear time and again from people who had lost all their hope. Mary, and Martha, the centurion, and Jairus. It is the cry of humanity reaching out into the very presence of God!

It was a cry served in a plate of faith garnished with grief and sprinkled with hope!

If only Jesus would come to his house, his boy would be made well!

Jesus answers him, *"Go your way, your son lives!"*

And John says that the man believed, and he went his way. . .period!

No arguments, no begging, no long discussions about the cause of the disease, no one calling anyone a puppy dog, no plea for an increase in faith, no falling down at the feet of Jesus, no praises, no immediate miracle, no walking down to a pool, no tears of joy. . . .nothing!

The *"Basilikos"* believed and went away! Period! No fanfare! He would not know for twenty-four hours whether his son was alive or dead! For all purposes, his son was dead! He would have to wait for almost twenty-four agonizing hours in pain, doubt, and confusion. His faith would have to hang on to the promise of the *Life Giver!* He would have to wait for the servants to tell him the *next day, "Yesterday, between 12 noon and 1 p.m., the fever left him!"*

The entire household believed in Jesus! Another soul and his family are drawn to the throne of mercy.

Let me leave you with one thought. . .

Come Lord, my son is dying.
Come Lord, this world is dying.
Come Lord, I am dying.

It would be the cry that would never go unanswered by the Creator God. It does not matter who you are. Rich or poor, blind or deaf or demon possessed, Jew or Gentile, male or female—that cry from a heart broken with sorrow and crushed by the fear of the inevitable and the unknown, is never left without an answer. In Him was life and a *"Basilikos"* searched for Him and took hold of that life at the risk of being killed by Herod!

Faith saw through a darkness that lasted twenty-four hours!

"Go your way, your son lives!"

Period!

27

"You Are Cordially Invited"

γαμος

Nearby stood six stone water jars, the kind used by the Jews for ceremonial washing, each holding from twenty to thirty gallons.
John 2:6 (NIV)

"*Baruch Atah HaShem MeSame'ach Chatan Im Hakalah*" *(You are blessed O Lord who makes the bridegroom and the bride rejoice together).*

: Dancing bridesmaids and joyful music of harps, lyre, *kinnor, nevel, timbrel,* and the sounds of the *shofar filled the sleepy little town of Cana.* They have waited for a whole year. The bridegroom had gone for a year after the betrothal and had prepared the house for her. Now he returns in the nighttime, with torches aflame and the noise of singing and jubilation and dancing bridesmaids in colorful clothes. Excitement fills the air as the retinue of bridesmaids and the community snake their way through the joyous village streets and approach her house. He returns to the house of the bride, riding a white horse.

Her waiting heart skips a beat as she hears the news that he has returned to take her with him.

Had they only known that heaven was in attendance, there would have been nothing lacking! This was not just an ordinary wedding set in some obscure village in Galilee. This was a wedding to which the Son of God was invited. Heaven would be watching, and so would the demons of hell!

She remembers the dowry that her father and he had agreed a year back. She remembers the covenant sealed with wine! She remembers the ring that was given her according to the laws of *Moshe and Israel!* She remembers the contract for the wedding. She remembers the *"Shiddukhin,"* the engagement! She remembers when a year ago he had promised her with these words: *"I am going away, and I will return when the house I have prepared for us is ready!"* She had waited with a veil over her face to signify that she was betrothed to him and none else. She had kept herself pure and blameless like Rachel had for Jacob! She hears the sound of music piercing the velvet Galilean night and brings out that unblemished robe, that wedding gown she had looked at and tried on a hundred times for this special moment in her life! The waiting is over! No more separation and no more yearning and wishing and hoping. No more loneliness spent in silence. She rushes to the door, flings open the door, and sees his silhouette on the white horse bathed in the flames of a thousand torches! There is her beloved.

"Arise, my darling,
my beautiful one, and come with me.
See! The winter is past;
the rains are over and gone.
Flowers appear on the earth;
the season of singing has come,
the cooing of doves
is heard in our land.
Arise, come, my darling;
my beautiful one, come with me." He cries! She dared not wait!

156

Ah! What a beautiful picture! Let the party begin! The wedding party would last for seven wonderful days, filled with joyous celebration, feasting and food, dancing and music. It was a challenge for any wedding coordinator. The seven blessings (*the Barachot*) need to be recited, and wine would freely flow each day as the bride and the groom are toasted over and over again by their closest family. The seven days of honeymooning would start for the couple as the family and friends celebrated this blessed occasion for seven days of feast and fun and dancing and happiness!

You would have expected Jesus, the Son of God, to have done a *"wow"* miracle as His announcement to the world that God was in the world, reconciling lost souls. *Not so!* It is in a humble wedding in an obscure little village that Jesus bursts forth into public ministry. The first miracle is none of the great ones; it is not a command given to raise Lazarus from the grave, nor is it the stilling of the storm at the lake, the healing of the blind and the deaf and the mute, nor is it the feeding of the 15,000 by a little boy's lunch, nor is it the casting away of the demons of hell. Nor is it a conflict between Beelzebub and the prince of angels! Instead the *magnum opus* is a wedding, a wedding in which the covenantal drink had run out!

Can you imagine running out of wine, which was used to bless the bride and the groom for seven days? No wine would mean no celebrations!

Jesus was at the wedding.

It was only day three! There were still four more days left of the wedding celebrations. Since Jesus was *"invited"* to the wedding, the couple must have been related to Jesus! Jesus was among His "earthly" relatives. He had to be very careful as to what miracle he performed. A little slip and a wrong move and He would be misunderstood, gossiped about, rejected, and thrown out.

His ministry had barely started. He was called, sent for, and directed to come here. His presence was somehow needed. He was one of the guests who was in the list of the wedding couple. That only meant one thing. The bride and the groom and their families must have known the family of Jesus. *They regarded Jesus important enough to want Him in their wedding.* That says a lot. There was a wedding, and He would be there. What a glorious experience. However, He would be three days late! Perfect timing!

Jesus, God Incarnate, Word of God, Son of the Most High, Immanuel, Prince of Peace, Counselor, Almighty God was invited to a wedding. This was the only wedding that He would attend while He was on this earth, and only John the Revelator would record this miracle. No one else would! There was no room for error, misunderstanding, or betrayal. He would come to the wedding and honor this couple with His presence.

Heaven would march into that earthly celebration. God was present at this wedding! God would personally grace the only wedding since the Garden of Eden. Genesis starts with a wedding, and Jesus' ministry starts with a wedding! And it would be in a wedding that John, the same author, would close the book of Revelation. Wonder if the couple even had the slightest idea as to who was coming to this wedding! Had they only known that heaven was in attendance, there would have been nothing lacking! This was not just an ordinary wedding set in some obscure village in Galilee. This was a wedding to which the Son of God was invited. Heaven would be watching, and so would the demons of hell!

The wedding coordinator had not planned well! Something just did not add up. And there was a problem. *A big problem!* There was no wine! They had run out of one of the most important ingredients in the wedding. *Wine! Better to have too much than too little!* The significance of the lack of wine in a wedding was beyond understanding. It bordered on negligence! It was the custom at that time, as it is today, not to run out of food or wine. That would mean a lack of respect, poor planning, upset guests and family, and humiliation for the family that conducted the wedding. Words would be exchanged for a long time in the synagogues and in other weddings around Galilee that what happened here at Cana should not and would not be repeated ever again! Jesus could not risk that.

What if He chose not to perform this miracle for His family and went ahead and performed all the rest of the miracles? This nightmare would hound Him for the rest of His three-and-a-half year ministry and His family would not forgive and would distance themselves from Him. *"Couldn't He have helped out in a wedding?"*

"He helped total strangers, He couldn't even respect the desires and the request of His mother!" He could not jeopardize that. Too many bigger and more important miracles were still ahead! This was his opportunity to *"help out"* in the wedding even though His time had not come! It was a time of crisis for those coordinating the wedding, and Jesus would succumb to the pleadings of His mother, Mariam!

She tells the servants, *"Do whatever He says!"* She knew that her Son was special.

Jesus commands, *"Fill up these ceremonial stone jars with water! Now draw some out and take it to the master of the feast!"*

And He prays: *"Baruch Atah Adonai, elohaynu melaech ha'olam boray pri ha'gafen..."* (*Praised are You Adonai our God, Sovereign of the Universe, who creates the fruit of the vine...)*

Water becomes wine...*That's it!*

Not just a cup or a glass of wine. Jesus changes gallons and gallons of water into wine! Six water pots, each of which could hold between 80–120 liters of water! 720 liters of the best grape juice this side of heaven!

The festivities continue as everyone rejoices in the simplicity of this miracle at the wedding!

What is interesting is the postlude to this miracle. John does not say that the servants, the master of ceremonies, Mariam, the newlywed couple or any of the wedding guests believed in Him. John simply states *"His disciples believed in Him...and they did not stay in Capernaum for many days!"* Was it a miracle solely for the benefit of the disciples? We would never know!

Let me leave you with this one thought! Somewhere in the heart of the Orion nebula, amidst the flashes of celestial fireworks and quasars, and the nursery of new stars and planets, the groom and his entourage are getting ready for a wedding of heavenly proportions, and you are invited! *"I will come again and take You unto Myself...I am going to prepare mansions for you...the marriage of the lamb has come, and His Bride has made herself ready...Blessed are those who are called to the marriage supper of the lamb...I saw heaven opened and behold a white horse and He who sat on him was called Faithful, and true...The armies of heaven followed*

Him. . .And I John saw the Holy city coming down from heaven as a bride adorned for her husband. . ."

There is a wedding, and you are invited to the wedding of Jesus and His Bride, the Church!

You are cordially invited to the wedding of Jesus the Son of God, the Lamb of God, the Husband of those that have been sealed with the blood of the Lamb! RSVP to the Holy Spirit before the end your days!

And nothing will run out in this wedding! There will be plenty of food and *wine!*

A little explanation would help!

Good wine sparkles and has alcohol in it! Note! In the wedding at Cana, they had four more days of "partying!" If Jesus had made alcoholic wine, and the people had consumed approximately 720 liters (each of the stone jars could roughly hold 80–120 liters of water. There were six of them!) of this alcoholic beverage, there would have been a lot of "drunk" people around. One liter contains roughly 33–35 ounces. That would mean that those six ceremonial stone water pots contained 23,760 ounces of wine which would provide a staggering 3,000 glasses of wine. That would equate to 3,000 ounces of pure unadulterated alcohol. Jesus would have performed a miracle that would have provided this wedding party with "heavenly alcohol!" As a general rule, 8 ounces of wine contains one ounce of pure alcohol. One ounce of alcohol can roughly correlate to .02 blood alcohol content (BAC). So four glasses of wine would equal a BAC of .08, which would make one legally drunk! The first miracle of Jesus, the Son of God would have been the cause of drunkenness, providing a wedding feast with 3,000 ounces of pure heavenly alcohol! I don't think so!

Would heaven have risked the chance that someone, just one person at the wedding, could have gotten drunk and become abusive? The demons of hell would have had a field day! God would have been misunderstood by the unfallen beings! Would the Word that became Flesh in the first chapter cause drunkenness in the second chapter of John? What does the Bible say about "wine"? The Greek word, "oinos" that is used in John, can be understood both as fermented or unfermented grape juice. So that does not help us any. So we seek contextual help from the Bible and see if the Bible actually condones the use of alcoholic wine.

Is Jesus contradicting the Old Testament by performing this bold and loud miracle in front of his immediate family and being the cause of drunkenness? Hardly!

Is He telling us that it is all right to drink alcohol? Absolutely not!

Has he sanctioned the use of fermented wine in weddings? Of course not!

Has God ever caused drunkenness? Never!

So, I have placed seventy-five biblical references to the consumption of fermented wine. Read it prayerfully and you decide!

There is more Scripture condemning the use of alcoholic beverages than will be found on the subjects of lying, adultery, swearing, cheating, hypocrisy, pride, or even blasphemy.

"Who has woe? Who has sorrow?
Who has strife? Who has complaints?
Who has needless bruises? Who has bloodshot eyes?
Those who linger over wine,
who go to sample bowls of mixed wine.
Do not gaze at wine when it is red,
when it sparkles in the cup,
when it goes down smoothly!
In the end it bites like a snake
and poisons like a viper.
Your eyes will see strange sights
and your mind imagine confusing things.
You will be like one sleeping on the high seas,
lying on top of the rigging." Prov 23: 29–34

Below are the reasons why I don't drink alcoholic wine!
Check it out yourself.

Gen 9:20–26. 19:30–38. Lev 10:9–11. Num 6:3. Deut 21:20; 29:5–6; 32:33. Jud 13:4, 7, 14. 1 Sam 1:14–15; 25:32–38. 2 Sam 11:13; 13:28–29. 1 Kings 16:8–10; 20:12–21. Esther 1:5–12. Psalm 75:8. Prov 4:17; 20:1; 23:19–20; 23:21; 23:29–30; 23:31; 23:32–35;

31:4–5; 31:6–7. Eccl 2:3; 10:17. Isa 5:11–12, 22; 19:14; 22:12–13; 24:9; 28:1,3,7,8; 56:9–12. Jer 35:2–14. Ezek 44:21. Dan 1:5–15; 5:1,2,3,23. Hos 4:11; 7:5. Joel 1:5, 3:3. Amos 2:8,12. Micah 2:11. Nahum 1:10. Hab 2:5,15,16. Matt 24:48. Luke 1:15; 12:45; 21:34. Rom 13:13; 14:21. 1 Cor 5:11; 6:10. Gal 5:21. Eph 5:18. 1 Thess 5:6–7. 1 Tim 3:2–3; 3:8,11. Titus 1:7–8; 2:2–3. 1 Peter 4:3–4.

God never contradicts Himself. The Word which became flesh and dwelt amongst us, made wine in a wedding at Cana. It was good tasting fresh grape juice, from the fruit of the vine, unfermented with heaven's blessing!

28

"Gone Fishing!"

υπαγω αλιευειν

*"I'm going out to fish," Simon Peter told them, and they said,
"We'll go with you." So they went out and got into the boat, but
that night they caught nothing.*
John 21:3 (NIV)

W e were tired!
All night long we had trolled the waters of this lake for fish.
We couldn't find a single *biny,* or a *musht* or a *sardine* to grace our
net! *Nothing!* Not even a dead sardine drifted into our nets. Fishing
is hard work. You could predict the seasons and the times that the
fish appeared on these waters, but you could never be sure where
the fish were. You depended on the gods to help you catch fish!
The boat beside yours would catch everything, while your net might
be totally and completely empty. At times I wondered why I was
fishing. But fishing sort of gets into your blood, and I had a whole
family that was into fishing. In fact, we had a whole fleet of boats,
and our family was well into the business! We had our ups and
downs. We had those days when we caught a lot and sometimes we
caught nothing!

> *The cold spray of the waves and the whisper of the gentle wind and the dancing reflection of the moon on the dark waters of the waveless sea was almost magical.* It was mesmerizing and healing. I had missed being a fisherman.

There are three kinds of nets that you used. The first was the *cast net*. As the name implies, you cast the nets from the shore. It was weighed down with rocks. It was circular, about twenty feet in diameter. You stood in waist high water and cast this net, and as the net sank to the bottom, you caught the fish, closed the net, and pulled the net like a purse to trap the fish inside. This was used for fishing from the shore.

The second type of net was the *drag net*. One end of the net would be held by your friends on the shore while you rowed the boat to a distance. And your friends would drag the net and thus catch what was available close to the shore.

The last method of fishing was the *trammel net*. This was what we mostly used. The net was held by a long beam of wood, and it dragged the lake. You let the net down and rowed. Whatever was in the water around you, you were able to catch. Since Lake Galilee contained *"schools"* of fish, this method was a guaranteed success. You only depended on the location of the fish and the brute strength of your rowing capabilities. You hardly used a single rod to catch fish when you are fishing for commercial purposes. But today was hard! Difficult!

It was one of those *nothing* days!

Too many events have occurred these past few weeks. The trial, the servant girl's accusations by the Roman fire that cold Friday morning, the rooster and my denials, Judas' suicide, Jesus' crucifixion, His resurrection, and His appearance in the upper room! I was still trying to wrap my head around all this. This was too much for a simple, uneducated fisherman like me to understand. I wish He had not died! I needed to understand Him. I could barely read. How was I ever to comprehend the meaning of the Messiah and the mission of Jesus? I recounted to Mark all that I could remember about the Lord, and he wrote them in his book! Who was this man

Jesus who had taken a rough and a mean fisherman like me and made me kind and compassionate?

I had spent only *three-and-one-half years* with Him. I really don't know who He is. He was loving and forgiving, and He had time for everyone. Even a prostitute who was caught in the act of this grave sin found peace and safety in Him. There was a time I saw Him with *Moses* and *Elijah* on a mountain. There was even a time when He called me the *Rock!* Me a *"Rock."* I am more like the sand that is on the shores of this sea, a constant irritation! I am an angry, foul mouthed, impatient fisherman. I could never argue like Him or I could never speak like Him! I could never be compassionate like Him! Me, Peter, a *"Rock"*. . .that was laughable!

I needed some time to clear my head and take hold of my bearings. The only place where I found peace was in the sea, the Sea of Tiberius. The only friends I connected with were these rough and hardy fishermen. They understood me! They were my family. I needed time, and I needed my old friends. I really do not know who this Jesus is! He had burst into my life like the sudden squalls that appear on these waters, and He has disappeared without any trace. When you are in the squalls, it is violent and troublesome and unpredictable, just like those three-and-one-half years I spent with Him.

I got on the boat. You know the favorite one with the blue and crimson paint. Thomas and Nathaniel, the sons of Zebedee and two other followers of Jesus came with me. It felt wonderful to unfurl that single mast and put my strong shoulders to the oar. The cool evening breeze from the hills above filled the patched-up, sea-worn sail. My mind raced with excitement. I was in my element! I knew these waters like the fish market at Capernaum. The fixed North Star guided me! We were off to catch some fish. This would do me good!

It was I who defended Him at Gethsemane. Yet it was I who denied Him three times! Three times! Cursed at Him! How could I have done this horrible thing? I was there at the cross, and I ran to the empty tomb. I was there when we saw Him in the upper room! Tears well up in my eyes. . .*God, how I miss Him! I just shook my head as I rowed with a renewed strength!*

The cold spray of the waves and the whisper of the gentle wind and the dancing reflection of the moon on the dark waters of the waveless sea was almost magical. It was mesmerizing and healing. I had missed being a fisherman. I had so much to learn and unlearn! These three-and-one-half years had been difficult, very difficult and exhausting. *I needed a break!*

We fished. All night long we fished. I went to all the special places where I was sure I would find some fish. Have I lost my sense of fishing? Have I lost my touch? *Have I been so long with Him that I had forgotten my trade?* Doubt, anger, and frustration tugged at my heart and tore at my inner spirit. This was humiliating. I was known as the big fisherman who always had a full boat of fish at the end of a day. *Not today!* How frustrating. All night long I searched my soul! I was angry at myself for having followed Him. I was angry because I had left all to follow a dream, a mirage, a distant story. I had walked miles with Him. I had argued with Him and protected Him. I even drew the sword in the Garden! Now He was gone! Where was He? Was the resurrection just a figment of my imagination? I wish He were here to answer my questions. I felt worthless, useless, and impotent! I couldn't even love myself! I couldn't even fish! What was I good for? *Nothing!*

The dark and starry night sky gently blushed as the eastern horizon turned pink, grey, and purple as sea gulls woke up another morning! It was time to turn home. The emptiness of the boat reflected my own emptiness. I was tired, exhausted, beaten, and disappointed. I was completely humiliated. I would be the laughing stock of all my friends. We had no fish! How disappointing! We neared the shore line.

It was then I saw a small smoky fire on the shore and a voice hailed us. *"Throw your net on the right side of the boat and you will find some fish!"* Who was this that is telling me a seasoned fisherman how to fish and where to cast my net. Did this person not realize who He was talking to? I was in no mood for some *"advice"* from someone on the beach, telling me where to cast my net. In defiant desperation I flung the cast net on the right side of the boat. The net began to quiver. I could not hold it in my hands *Fish!* They were all over the net! My net came alive as a hundred—no, a hundred and fifty-three fish to be exact—splashed around in the net. The spray of the fish in the net glistened like pink topaz in the early morning twilight! I was amazed! How did this man on the shore know where the fish were! It was then that John spoke up. *"Peter, it is the Lord!"*

Excitement, joy, confusion, release of pent-up anger, and frustration that was bottled up inside me exploded when I saw and recognized Jesus, my Jesus, at the shore. The fish had to wait. I jumped into the water and swam to the shore and fell at my Master's feet with tears running down my cheek!

He fed us a meal of bread and fried fish. Then He asked me a question three times that cut through my heart, just like those three times I had denied Him around a similar early morning fire in a Roman courtyard: *"Simon, son of Jonah, do you love me?"*

That was almost thirty years ago.

So much has changed since then! I am a prisoner now.

The dungeons of Mamertine in Rome have been my home!

I am old! I can barely see. My body is bent with age, but my mind is clear! I remember Matthew, Thomas, Andrew, Philip. . .one by one we heard that they were killed in some strange distant land.

John is exiled to the salt mines of Patmos.

It is my turn today! I am to be crucified when the sun rises!

My mind wanders to another sunrise. . .

I see Him walking towards me on the Galilean shore.

He speaks,

"Simon son of Jonah, do you love me?
Simon son of Jonah do you love me?
Simon son of Jonah, do you love me?"

The sound of footsteps shatters the silence!
A key unlocks the prison door!
It is time! They have come for my crucifixion!
I struggle to my feet and whisper my answer heavenward!
"Yes Lord. You know that I love You."

29

Lazarus

λαζαρος

After he had said this, he went on to tell them, "Our friend Lazarus has fallen asleep; but I am going there to wake him up."
John 11:11 (NIV)

My name is Miriam. I live in the obscure village of Bethany, two miles from Jerusalem, the City of David, with my brother *Elyazar* and my sister *Martha*. Jesus and his friends spent a lot of time with us. They did not like to stay in Jerusalem, and we offered them our home whenever they came this way. What are friends for? And besides, He was always kind towards the less fortunate among us. He healed the blind, the lame, and the sick. He was well-liked by the poor and hated by the obstinate Pharisees and the teachers of the Law. They could not understand Him and did not want Him anywhere near Jerusalem. They were intimidated by His popularity and were plotting His death!

Bethany, our village was very close to Mt. Olives and to the garden of Gethsemane! The hillside was green and covered with olive groves, palm trees, and fig trees! We called our village *"Home of the Afflicted!"* Some called it, *"Home of the dates!"* due to the abundance of dates that was available nearby.

Since the sick and the afflicted could not *"live"* in Jerusalem, the Holy City, they were forced to live in the groves and orchards. That's right! The leaders of Jerusalem even made a rule that unclean lepers could not be anywhere near the City of David! There were so many rules and regulations regarding the preservation of the Holy City that the people who were sick had no chance to even visit Jerusalem.

> *I wanted nothing to do with Him. What good is He to us now? My brother was dead! Martha went to meet Him. I stayed home drowning in my sorrow and lost in my betrayal by Him!*

They had to look for other accommodations. The closest city within walking distance was *Bethany!* Of course you could sneak into the city and risk the chance of death! So needless to say, the little tiny village was a stopover for the sick, the dying, and the unclean foreigners!

Jerusalem, on the other hand, housed the people of wealth and nobility. The scribes, the teachers of the Law, the Roman dignitaries, the high priest, the Pharisees, and the Sadducees lived within the walls of the neatly manicured and exceptionally clean and groomed city. Herod's Temple, a testament to the opulence of what the kingdom of Solomon once was, was the heartbeat of Jerusalem. There was one place where the unwanted could gather, and that was at the Pool of Bethesda. But, that is a different story for another time! If you had money and wealth, Jerusalem was your destination. If you were poor and of ill repute, Bethany was your watering hole!

The traders skipped our little town. Who had money to buy those expensive wares that these "merchants" peddled? We barely had money to buy food. Who could afford to buy gold from Ophir, silk from the East, fine linen from Egypt, myrrh and the frankincense and the exotic spices from distant lands, ivory from Ethiopia, and precious stones from Solomon's mines? But over the years I had scrounged and saved some money and had gotten some sweet-smelling expensive nard from one of the merchants of the East. Now that was my only prized possession.

Well, these merchants knew that there was money to be made in the temple and in Jerusalem, not here in Bethany. Of course when these caravans passed through our town, we would all gather outside and watch with wonder and amazement at the grunting, colorful camels with muffled bells and the mysterious traders from the East who commandeered these ships of the desert. These men were the golden-daggered children of *Ishmael.* Ruddy brown and weathered by the desert, they wore colorful turbans and stared at you with piercing brown eyes that have seen a thousand sandstorms in the hot desert. Those eyes burned a hole through your heart! The Nabateans from the pink city who traveled through King Solomon's way and came through the desert of *Wadi Rum,* also passed through our little village. They in turn brought in the spices and precious stones, expensive copper pots, and fancy jewelry and linen from the ships that traded from far-off countries.

It was obvious that no one trusted anyone! These men, the children of Ishmael were our distant cousins who were the traders and the providers of that which we needed daily for the temple services. They provided the temple priests with pure frankincense and myrrh that was used in the prayers at Herod's Temple. *It was obvious that somehow YHWH had connected the children of Ishmael with the children of Jacob.* Without the incense from the Ishmaelites, there would be no temple services, and they were the only ones who could provide the purest and the sweetest frankincense. YHWH demanded the best, and the Ishmaelites took pride in providing the best, most expensive frankincense. It was a relationship of necessity, which involved money!

What was almost laughable was that even though these traders from Egypt, Babylon, and Petra converged on the city of David, they were not allowed to spend the nights there. They were deemed *"unclean!"* So they would camp on the outsides of the city, along with the sick and the dying, close to Bethany. Their campfires would be a testament to the *"purity"* that was manifest in Jerusalem. Often at nighttime, strange-sounding music, punctuated with tambourines, flutes, drums, and high-pitched voices, would stab the hills around Bethany. We would also hear the eerie wail of families as they lost the battle of their loved ones to the clutches of death's ever-expanding claws.

Our family was poor but happy. Our needs were simple, and we were satisfied if we had a table with some bread, goat cheese, olives, dates, dried figs, some radishes, and dried fish. Bethany subsisted on necessities and not on opulence. When your time came and you got sick, that was it. All the physicians were in Jerusalem where they could make money and charge exorbitant prices for their medicine. We dared not trust the potions peddled by the traders, these sons of Ishmael, to cure any disease! Here in Bethany, death was a common occurrence. People died everyday. You just waited your turn. You were poor, and that was a reality. It was a village full of sick people with no one to heal! We lived in this town, a town that was touched by disease, sickness, death, and wealthy traders from the desert: such a wild, strange and a colorful contrast!

One day *Elyazar,* our only beloved brother, got sick. You see we were a tight-knit family. We had each other, and that was enough. There was just me, Martha, and *Elyazar.* That was it. Having my brother around gave us protection, comfort, and a sense of belonging. He would one day get married, and our family would grow, and, maybe like Abraham, we too might move away from this little village and set our roots somewhere else, and our family would be as numerous as the stars of heaven. *Elyazar meant "God is my help!" Little did I know at that time that God would be his ONLY help!*

What started as a simple cough developed into fever and chills. Martha and I tried everything to heal our brother. We made a concoction of crushed myrrh, garlic, fennel, borage, pomegranate tarragon, hyssop, and blackberry. We strained it and treated him with it. That was the popular medicine. *But nothing happened.* He only got worse. Jesus wasn't too far away, and we decided that since He can heal those who are sick, maybe He would come and heal His friend. Jesus and His disciples had been to our house on numerous occasions, and we had housed, fed, and taken care of all of them. I knew that if we sent word to Jesus, surely He would come and heal Lazarus.

We sent word.

He never came.

And Lazarus died.

Wish Jesus would have come!

Death is so brutal! It is such a final separation! We washed our brother's body and placed spices and fragrant oils all around it. The same day, we laid *Elyazar's* cold body on a bed of salt and closed his eyes. We made sure that his hair was trimmed and his nails were clipped for that great resurrection day when He would come forth from the grave. He looked so peaceful in death. How he would tease us and throw rocks at us! Those eyes that used to sparkle with mischief and love were now silent! We had played and laughed and cried and loved each other. His strong frame had been our only protection. *Now he was dead! Ah! I can't go on! If only I could have died in his stead!*

We then secured his jaw with a piece of linen and wrapped his body in pure white linen that we had bought from one of the traders from Egypt. We laid his body on a wooden pallet and carried it to our family tomb outside Bethany. Martha and I and a number of women led the funeral procession, crying and beating our chests, wailing as only sisters knew how! He was our blood, our security, our brother. He was now gone. How we loved *Elyazar!* The men carried the body and followed in silence. They were responsible for birth and they were held accountable for death. *Where was Jesus? He was supposed to have been here! Days ago we had sent messengers to him!*

Jesus and His friends did not even come to the funeral! How rude! Our custom demanded reciprocity. Not even a word of condolence from *Him. He had talked about being kind and loving and merciful. He had shown kindness to strangers and had healed a thousand ungrateful people who would have killed Him in a heartbeat! Here we were, His closest friends. . .and. . .and. . .and. . .He did not even have the courtesy to come for the funeral! We had fed them and housed them when we had nothing! I don't understand Him! What kind of a man is He! What a hypocrite! I hope I never see Him again!*

I agonized over my own anger and frustrations. Something was not right! He was contradicting everything that He had said.

Four long and agonizing days have passed since we buried Elyazar in the family tomb. I was angry!

There was a knock at the door; a little boy came bursting through the door! "Jesus is here, on the outskirts of the city!" he blurted out!

I wanted nothing to do with Him. What good is He to us now? My brother was dead! Martha went to meet Him. I stayed home drowning in my sorrow and lost in my betrayal by Him!

"He is asking for you!" Martha came back and told me.

I was numb with pain and sorrow and anguish!

It took all my energy to gather myself and go to this man who had so publicly humiliated us by His absence!

"Lord, if you had been here, my brother would not have died." I screamed at Him, angrily! I wish I could have slapped Him! My anger knew no bounds, and my sorrow had no confines!

He whispered ever so gently, "Where have you laid him?"

"Come and see, Lord," I replied! Yes, you need to see your friend's tomb!

I lifted my head and looked into those gentlest of eyes. Through my own bleary angry tear stained eyes I saw Him. His eyes were filled with tears. He was weeping! It felt strange! Couldn't He have stopped all this? I knew He could have healed Elyazar!

We took Him to the tomb!

A crowd of onlookers, traders, strangers, and the sick followed us to the tomb!

Elyazar was dead for *four days*. Four days! The Rabbi's had taught us that for three days the soul of the dead hovered around the dead body and tried to enter it. On the fourth day, since the body had changed, the soul was unable to recognize the body and would fly away! We reminded the master *two* times that he was dead for four days! *Elyazar* had been in the grave for four days! Four long and dreadful days! Even his soul would be unable to recognize him! We were required to mourn for seven days. And then after one year, we would open the grave, collect his remaining bones, sweep them to a corner, and wait for the next funeral and the next body to occupy the family tomb. It was all so sad and heartbreaking. Why did my brother have to die! *Why? Why? Why? My heart was broken into a million pieces!*

*Then He said something that was profane! "Roll away the stone!"
What? Why would He want to do that? His words cut through my
own grieving body like hot coals on a cold night!*

It has been four days, and my brother's body would be rotting!

*The heat of Bethany and the windowless tomb were a perfect
combination for the putrefaction of a dead body!*

*The stench would be horrible! Even the soul would have by now
fled in terror!*

*Why would He want to humiliate us like this! Was it not
enough that Elyazar was dead? You only opened the tomb a year
later, AFTER the body was completely decomposed and only the
bones remained! Never in Bethany or anywhere in Israel had
anything like this happened. You just do not open up a grave
while the body was rotting! That would be humiliating for the
family and the talk of this miserable village and all of Jerusalem.
We would be unable to live in this town! Such gossip and. . .
"Lazarus! Come forth!"*

*The voice of Jesus cut through my self-pity and seared through
my own questions! I could not believe my ears! Did I hear right?
All eyes were on the entrance to that tomb! I could not believe what
I saw: my brother's body was walking silently from the darkness of
the tomb to the sunlight where the Master was!*

*I did not know what to do! "Take off the grave clothes and free
him!" I heard Him say!*

*My brother, my only brother who was dead was alive. . .Jesus
had called him from the grave. He had made the words*

"O death where is thy sting!

O grave where is thy victory" a REALITY!

*I was speechless! I ran to the tomb! My brother who was dead
was alive! My heart exploded into song and praise! Where once
there was anger, sorrow, and frustration, there sprung up gratitude,
joy, and exhilaration. Only God could do that! Only God could call
a putrefying dead body back to life!*

*In my desperation I forgot that we were the object of one of the
most important miracles that heaven would perform on this earth. . .*

Let me leave you with one thought:

I was the one who washed His feet with the expensive perfume at *Simon's house*.

I stood in the shadows when the mob cried, *"Crucify Him!"*

I was at the *Hill of the Skull,* when the Romans nailed Him to a wooden cross!

I helped *Joseph of Arimethea* take His dead body from the cross.

I was at the *tomb* early on Sunday.

I heard Him call me *" Mary" at the garden.*

It was to me that He *first* appeared after the crucifixion!

I was the first witness to the *Resurrection of Jesus the Messiah,* the Son of God, the Keeper of Israel, The Only One who can call the dead back to life! He called my brother from death's sleep!

I would never be the same! This is *my* testimony!

I was there!

30
"I Am the Man!"

εγω ειμι

He replied, "The man they call Jesus made some mud and put it on my eyes. He told me to go to Siloam and wash. So I went and washed, and then I could see."
John 9:11 (NIV)

It was the Holy Sabbath Day! Even we knew the laws! There were thirty-nine categories of work that were prohibited on the Sabbath. How you prepared bread, the dress you wore, how you wrote, where you traveled, and how you kept your private house...all had "special" Sabbath Laws!

I am blind! I was born blind! I am a beggar! I will beg by the walls of Jerusalem until the day I die. No hope! No future! Exiled from the land of the living, I will rot in this valley and one day join the dust out of which I was made. *Not soon enough!* Who enjoyed living in the dark? Who lived on the mercies of strangers to give you your next meal? You could not let your guard down even once! You might get trampled upon, beat up, mugged, or even get killed! I was the scum of the earth, and people made sure that I had no illusions of grandeur! Blind beggars lived on the edge, and I was no exception!

Each beggar had staked his claim at one of the many gates that were the entry point to the city!

There were so many pools in Jerusalem. *There was the Sheep Pool (Pool of Bethesda), The Tower Pool, Israel Pool, The Serpent's Pool, and the Pool of Siloam!*

The Pool of *Bethesda* was on one end of the city by the Temple

No one could heal a blind man! Come on, that meant that someone would have to create two eyes and place them in these two hollow sockets! *How likely is that to happen?*

and the Pool of *Siloam* was at the other end of the city by the *Valley of Hinnom*, close to the house of Caiaphas, the high priest! The Pool of Siloam was at the place where the *Valley of Hinnom* and the *Kidron Valley* joined together. The road to the Salt Sea passed right through the pool, and it was an important place where people gathered to enjoy its cool waters before they traveled to the dry and hot Dead Sea. The pool was at the entrance to the Water *Gate* and stood at the tail end of the *Tyropoeon Valley,* which separated *Mount Moriah* from *Mount Zion*! King Hezekiah's tunnel connected the *Gihon* Spring in the *Kidron Valley* to the Pool of Siloam. It was an important historical pool that supplied cool and refreshing waters to those who entered or left Jerusalem. It was a center for gossip entering and leaving Lower Jerusalem!

My story involves the Pool of Siloam!

I already told you that I was *born* blind. That meant that I was cursed *before* I was conceived! I had not done anything to deserve this blindness. I was cursed while I was *being* conceived. *How could I have been responsible?* That blame obviously fell on my parents who conceived me, or so I thought! *How much worse can it get?* Not being able to see because you were *born* that way. It was not a disease or an accident that was the cause of these hollow sockets that graced my head! I was *born* that way! I had no control over my blindness!

How could an all merciful God who provided manna in the wilderness for forty years for *Moshe* and protected group of rebellious *slaves* who followed Him do this to me? Come on, I was even told that their slippers did not wear down for forty years! YHWH even healed *Naaman*, the Gentile from leprosy, and I am not that bad! And there was that story about the shepherd boy David, killing a mighty Philistine warrior with just a stone! *If* YHWH can do all that and *if* YHWH is so powerful and merciful, *why on earth did He create me without any eyes? Huh?* Answer that one! Makes no sense. Unless of course, there was no YHWH! Then all reasoning would be silent, and we would have to accept that there was no God! *No one could heal a blind man!* Come on, that meant that someone would have to create two eyes and place them in these two hollow sockets! *How likely is that to happen?* These physicians can't even heal a man with a simple cough and a fever and a boil on his back! Ridiculous!

I hear a commotion! I hear steps approaching me! I hear someone getting ready to spit. That guttural grunt that comes just before someone clears their throat; then there is silence! I feel warm oozy clay being slapped in my eye sockets. . . .Hey! Hold on! I never asked for clay to be placed in my eye socket! I struggle and flail my hands in front of my face and reach for that hand that has violated my privacy, as if I had any privacy left. I clutch at those hands in front of my face with anger! How dare anyone. . .I hear a voice, "Go wash in the Pool of Siloam!"

I had a thousand questions. . .Why? Why should I wash my face? Why should I go to the pool? Why not just wash here? Who was this man? Why is He doing something like this? Why is He humiliating a blind beggar like me? Why? Why? Why? I had neither asked this man for food nor had I begged him for money!

A hand gripped me and led me to the Pool of Siloam, in Lower Jerusalem! When you are blind you depended on the kindness of strangers! I did not know what to expect. I was told to wash! Of course I needed to get this oozy clay from my empty eye sockets. I almost tripped over the three steps that led down to the pool. I knelt down on the steps and splashed the cold water all over my face and my eyes. . .Whoa! Something was happening! My empty sockets were getting filled! The clay was getting harder! Should I even dare to open my eyes? Should I? What if I could actually see! But I had not asked to be healed! How would I adjust to my surroundings! A thousand questions scratched at my soul like the fleas on a hundred camels. I opened my eyes! The stabbing glare of sunlight pierced my darkness. I squinted my eyes and raised my hand to cover the brightness. Through the gap between my fingers I could see the blue waters of the pool dancing in the sunlight! I could see people and clothes and flowers and children and camels and the accusing look of the Pharisees and the temple guards!

They dragged me to their leader in the temple for washing my face on the Sabbath in a public pool! They did not even care that I was once blind and now I could see! They were so worried about their *Shabbat* they forgot that I was totally and completely restored! They did not believe my story that a prophet had healed me. Who would believe such a fairy tale? They said He was not a prophet and that He was a demon. They said that I broke the *Shabbat,* and so did He. They asked my parents if I was born blind.

They never believed my story. And then they brought me in a *second time* and told me. *"Give glory to God by telling the truth."* Even a beggar like me knew the grave finality of that statement. This is exactly what they told *Achan* before they stoned him for stealing some spoils of war. I knew what was coming next. If I acknowledged that, I would be stoned as well. I was not going to touch that statement. I was not going to give glory to anyone! If anyone needed any *"glorying"* it must be that Man who healed me!

I lashed out at them in anger! These blind teachers of the Law! *"How many times do I have to tell you this story? I was blind! Even my parents and my friends know that! I don't know who healed me. I know He must be a Prophet! He must be a Man sent from God! Do you want to become His disciples too?"* They were infuriated at my suggestion. They called me names and accused me of being a sinner, and they called the temple guards, and they *excommunicated me* from the temple! That was huge! Being excommunicated by the priests in Jerusalem meant that you could not atone for any sins, and you could not *ever* get inside the temple grounds to pray! Even my parents knew that I was a doomed and lost soul! Without the atonement for sins and the events of *Yom Kippur* and the festival days, you are a lost soul!

But who cares! I can now see! I was blind once, but *now* I can see! I was filled with joy and gladness. Those white-washed sepulchers can keep their temple to themselves! *Those so-called "sons of Avram" can rot in their synagogues!* I had lived in darkness since my birth, but now that Prophet had healed me. He had given me eyes to see, *a gift that I had longed for but never requested!* I now had a purpose and a meaning to my dark life! There was no one that would rejoice with me, not my parents, not the priests. No one! How sad! Later that day, He came looking for me. He found me by the pool. I was surrounded by fellow beggars who knew that I was born blind. I could not stop talking.

I was seeing faces, which once I had only heard!

"Do you believe in the Son of God?" He asked me.

"Who is it, Lord?" I asked

"You have seen Him, and it is He who is talking to you," He replied!

I fell face down at His feet. *"Lord, I believe!"*

I have seen God and now I can give Him the glory!

Can I say one thing as I close?

I don't know why He chose me! There was nothing special about me! I just sat in my misery day after day, year after year, surrounded by filth, dirt, and garbage! I never asked to be healed. I never begged anyone to give me eyes to see. Certainly not Him! I had with resignation accepted the fact that I was born blind and one day I would die blind. He never asked me if I wanted to see! He never asked me if I wanted a healing. He never explained what He was doing! He just presumed!

I did not give Him permission to stick that clay mixed with spit in my eyes! Why me? Why did He choose me out of all those blind beggars that infested the walls of Jerusalem! They were all blind, and they all needed a healing! Why was I singled out? Was I so special that God made a detour to reach me while He was on this earth? I was shown and blessed with unmerited favor I did not request or deserve! Could this be that this is what grace is? I had so many questions, and a lifetime to learn the answers!

Could it be that grace marches uninvited into the solitude of our lives, confronts us when we are at our lowest, explodes into the eclipse of our dark and doomed present, boldly restores us, and drops us speechless at the feet of Jesus?

That day I was excommunicated by the priests, but I was grafted into the family of God! He never once told me that I was a sinner or give me a reason why He healed me! He healed me first, and then He asked me to believe in Him!

I must have been very special!

That Shabbat, I, who was once blind, received grace, unmerited and unrequested favor! "Lord, I believe!"

(*Note: Jesus would perform seven very poignant miracles on the Shabbat! And this would infuriate the rabbis so much so that they plotted to get rid of Him. How sad!*

He would heal a lame man by the pool of Bethesda, John 5:1–18;
He would drive out an evil spirit Mark, 1:21–28;
He would heal Peter's mother-in-law Mark, 1:29–31;
He would heal a man with a withered hand, Luke 6:6;
He would heal a blind man, John 9:1–16;
A crippled woman would walk again! Luke 13:10–17;
A man with dropsy would live to see another day! Luke 14:1–6)

31
Eighteen Years

δεκαοκτω

On a Sabbath Jesus was teaching in one of the synagogues, and a woman was there who had been crippled by a spirit for eighteen years. She was bent over and could not straighten up at all.
Luke 13:10–11 (NIV)

One miracle, seen through the eyes of three people:
The Ruler of the Synagogue,
The Crippled Woman
and Jesus

1. The Ruler of the Synagogue:

*H*ow inconsiderate! He called me a "Hypocrite!" How dare *He? Why would He do something like this?* Why would He disrespect me in front of my own congregation? It almost seems that He was being confrontational! I had given Him the *privilege* to speak on the *Shabbat* at *my* synagogue. *My reputation was at stake.* I took a huge risk in allowing *Him* to speak! I knew His mother! I knew that He was a good man, and I knew that the people liked Him. I also knew that the religious leaders, especially Pharisees and the temple leaders despised Him. *I took a huge chance!* The reading was good. He had a great grasp on the subject of the Torah and the writings. I was mesmerized by His explanation of the various theological patterns that were sprinkled throughout the reading for the day. I was actually beginning to enjoy listening to this *ben-Yosef, the son of Joseph! And then this!*

> *If I were to meet God,* I would ask Him one question: *Why? Why did You make me like this?* I had not done anything to deserve this punishment. Look at me, God! *Are You there? Are You listening?*

If you looked at Him, you would think he was a very common-looking man. There was nothing special about His physique. He could have been the local shepherd or a carpenter like His father Joseph. He was rugged, wiry, traveled a lot, and was a good hard working young man. I had known Him for some time.

But when He took the Scrolls in His hands and placed the seamless purple and blue *Tallit* and started praying,

"Baruch Atah Adonai Elohaynu melech ha'olam asher bachar banu mikol ha'amim ve'natan lanu et torahto Baruch Atah Adonai notayn ha-Torah. . ."(Praised is Adonai our God, Sovereign of the Universe, who has chosen us from all the peoples by giving us Torah. Praised is Adonai, Giver of the Torah), something took over Him. It was like being in the presence of *Moshe* or even *Avram.* There was something about this *ben-Yoseph* that transcended all powers of reasoning. In His presence I felt humbled. It seemed that He could somehow look right through my façade as the *"Ruler of the Synagogue"* and see all my weaknesses and my goodness. I was transparent before Him. That is why it hurt so much when He called me a *hypocrite!* You see, in my heart I am a good man. I loved my people.

All I did was protect Him. I did not want Him to get into trouble. There were so many spies looking at Him, watching His every move. They would sell Him out to the leaders for a dirty silver coin. It was all about money and being in favor with the higher authorities. And besides, if they knew that I did not speak up and was condoning His activities of "healing and working" on the *Shabbat,* I would be in big trouble. They might even get rid of me and worse still, there might even be a riot as more sick people would be brought into the synagogue on the *Shabbat;* then the Romans would be brought in to chase these people out and to "keep the peace," and they would enter the synagogue and desecrate it, and that would be the end of this synagogue, my career, and my life. *I had to speak up!* What if a leper showed up inside the synagogue on the Sabbath day? That would desecrate everyone and the risks were too much. I was protecting *ben-Yosef,* my congregation, my community, the Shabbat Laws, my job, my life, and the words of the Torah written by Moshe himself. We cannot forget the *K'dushat HaYom* and its five elements. We have to remember that the Shabbat is God's *matanah* (gift). We have to remember that the Shabbat is an eternal *birith* (covenant). We have to remember to do *La'asot* (observe) the Shabbat. We have to remember that the Shabbat is a *oneg* (a delight), and finally we must not forget that YHWH Himself has *sanctified* this day, the queen of all days. I cannot, as the leader of my synagogue, allow unruly behavior on this day. There are other days to heal the sick. *The Shabbat is a special Holy Day.* That is why I spoke up and got reprimanded for defending the Shabbat and was called a hypocrite. *I don't get this!* How dare this unruly *ben-Yosef* accuse me in front of my congregation. *Does He think He is God?* I am overcome with anger!

2. The Sick Woman:

How Humiliating! Day after painful day I wander the streets or sit in my house alone, cursed by God and shunned by my own people. *I knew my place in the society.* I knew where I belonged. I was a nobody. One day this disease would overtake my life, and I would join the dust out of which I was created.

I was not born like this. I don't even *remember* how I got this disease. It slowly took over my spine and contorted the bones that formed my back. The disease twisted my body into an ugly shape. I could barely walk. I was in pain all the time. *Hunched over, rejected, cursed, an anomaly in my neighborhood, I was bruised and broken physically, mentally, and spiritually.*

If I were to meet God, I would ask Him one question: *Why? Why did You make me like this?* I had not done anything to *deserve* this punishment. Look at me, God! *Are You there? Are You listening?* For eighteen long years I have toiled, struggled just to walk, and had been constantly raked with agony. Why me? *What did I ever do to receive such a "blessing" from You?* All around me I see people who are normal and happy, with a family and full of laughter. My life was eclipsed by darkness in an eternal sunset. I lived in the shadows. Why me? I had no family, no loved ones; I was forsaken by all and rejected by those that once knew me. *I lived to die!*

The *Shabbat* was the only time I got to *"meet"* people. It was the only time I would have contact with others. I would sneak into the synagogue long before anyone would and find my special place in the back, away from all the people, and wait. It was wonderful to see children and women and families and hear all the gossip! It was even healing to be in the presence of the only place I knew where God would visit His people. He would come one day, and I would meet Him! *Ah! Only if that were true!* I enjoyed the teachings of the rabbi and the readings. I could not understand all the complicated words of the *Torah*. But it was enough to be in the presence of the *Torah*. I was just glad to be in the synagogue. It was almost like all my troubles and pains and problems disappeared. I was in the presence of God, even though I was angry at Him!

That *Shabbat* was like any other *Shabbat*. I snuck in and sat at the back, at the very back at my usual place along with the unwanted. You see, the front of the Synagogue was reserved for the special people, and the back was where the unwanted and the unclean sat! It was someone else who was reading the Torah. I looked up and saw that it was *ben-Yosef. I had heard that He had been healing people and restoring their eyesight and giving them food to eat.* I was captivated by His reading of the Torah. He read like no one I had heard all these years. I was mesmerized. *It almost sounded like He was reading something that He himself had written.* He had such a wonderful and a clear voice, laced with beautiful intonations and rhythm. The *Baruch* never sounded like this and the *shemay* sounded never sweeter. He then stared reading from the Prophet Isaiah, something about setting captives free. He closed the *Torah* and began to teach. We were spellbound and captivated. There was pin-drop silence as the voice of *ben-Yosef* bounced from rafter to wall to our ears. It sounded like God Himself was talking to us. It sounded like the sound of many waters, crystal clear, authoritative, dynamic; all eyes were on Him. My eyes locked into His. He stopped right in the middle of a sentence!

"Woman" He said pointing directly at me, *"come here!"*

Me? He wants me to come to Him! I looked around to make sure that He was talking to me. The hands of two beggars who were sitting next to me gently lifted my contorted body and led me to Him! There were soft murmurs as people turned their heads and saw who He had addressed!

He looked at me with compassion and sorrow, as if He were asking my forgiveness for those eighteen long years that I have been held captive! He gently laid His hands on me and said, *"You are now healed!"* Immediately a power surged through those bent and broken bones, and my back straightened. I was no longer a cripple. There were hushed voices at first and then praises as people began to understand what had taken place in front of their very own eyes! I, a woman who was sick in their presence for eighteen horrible years, was now made well. *Hallelujah!*

I met Him in His sanctuary, deformed or not, shunned or not, forsaken or not. Nothing would matter to Him. I spent my days in the synagogue until I was at peace with Him. I was at peace when He came my way! I had found my REST on the Day of Rest. From this day forth, the Shabbat would be my Day of Rest. It was on this day that I received rest from my terminal illness. He found me in the synagogue on the day of Rest, and He gave my tired, forgotten, deformed and sick soul rest.

And then He called me something that nobody had ever called me. He called me a "Daughter of Abraham". A daughter of promise. A daughter in the lineage of Abraham, Isaac, and Jacob. Hallelujah! Baruch Atah Adonai Elohim Israel! (Praise be to the Lord God of Israel!)

3. Jesus:

How heart wrenching! "My heart is in anguish within me. I see my Creation held in captive since that fateful day at the Garden of Eden. So much sorrow. So many tears. So many hearts broken and bleeding. So many lost souls left for dead as the enemy ravages them! The forces of darkness swirl around them with frenzied excitement. Gabriel has never left my side! My own army of angelic hosts accompany me and protect me as I travel these dusty roads.

Wars are fought each day. Battles are conducted with fierceness. Souls are destroyed. The enemy will not stop. He knows his time is short! I have entered the battlefield, and one day I will vanquish the powers of hell. I am in the presence of the one who has claimed this earth as his own. It is into the war zone of Lucifer and his angels that I have entered! They have been preparing for my visit! He will not relinquish. He will not give up without a fight, a fight that will take me to Golgotha and cost me separation from the Father and the Spirit! There is constant war and continued battle for each soul. My soul is filled with compassion for this small segment of people who are tortured and have been placed in dungeons of bondage.

Here I am in their synagogue, a place where they have gathered for centuries, their sanctuary. They have come to hear me! What can I say? What can I tell them? How can I reach them? If only their eyes could be opened they would see demons of hell and the angels of light fighting for their very souls. *O that my eyes were a fountain of waters that I might weep for these lost sons and daughters of Abraham.* I begin to read the words I told them on Mt. Sinai 1,500 years ago, the eternal everlasting words. They have clung to the words like drowning sailors clutching to a reed in a storm in the seas! *They have placed so many barriers and have bound and insulated themselves with so many layers of detailed regulations that they have lost the meaning of those words etched in Sinai's rocks!* What can I tell them? How can I show them? How can I lead them? Will they even listen?

I see her! I know her! I was there when she was conceived and birthed. I was present when she got sick! I was there fighting for her and her life. I have visited each of her dark chapters and read each of her anguished stories! *Her cries have reached the throne room of God. We had decided that she would be one of the people I would meet when I am on this earth!* Now she sits, forgotten, tired, in pain, miserable, and broken in spirit. *Only if she knew that today would be her day of deliverance!* I cannot go on reading the *Torah!* I cannot continue until she finds her rest! *The Shabbat rules would have to wait!* The *Torah would have to wait!* I look at her. My eyes hold her! I see the demons of hell around her. Those angels of darkness that have claimed her for eighteen long years dance around her in a frenzy! They know what will happen next. They have watched me at the tombs at Gergesa; they have seen me destroy them a thousand times. I knew them, and they knew me. They were there when Lucifer waged the war in heaven. They were there when I pled with them not to listen to him! They had now promised their allegiance to the prince of darkness! They scream and scratch and claw the air in front of her as if to protect her from my own army that is even now marching towards her. A fight for her very soul is now engaged. *I have come to claim that which was mine in the first place. This daughter of Abraham was mine. I created her, and I have redeemed her!*

I command her, *"Woman come here!"*

In order for me to set her free, she must respond to my invitation. The demons hold her down as she tries to respond. I see her guardian angel, the one that was with her since her birth, respond to my command! A pair of earthly hands help her. *Heaven cannot intervene in the process of human choice!*

She struggles to her feet as heaven's mightiest army encircles her and protects her from the screaming demons of hell and lead her to me! She reaches me surrounded by my own army, her own form lost in the flashes of heavens light that encircle her.

"You are healed!" The battle is over for that one lost daughter of Abraham, freed from the demons of hell after eighteen long years in agonizing captivity.

I look for words of comfort from the leader of the synagogue. *All I received were words of accusations for having violated the Shabbat!* My heart cries within me. *Even in victory, there is defeat!*

I melt into the shadows to fight another war as demons of hell dance in a synagogue on the day of rest! I am tired! I must get some rest!

"Come unto me all ye that are burdened and I will give you rest. . ." *even if it means that I might be misunderstood and accused and be blamed and finally be nailed to a Roman cross on a dark Friday and would cry out "Eloi, Eloi, Lamasachthani (My God! My God! Why have You forsaken Me!) I will give you rest, the Shabbat rest! Leave your worries and come to me!"*

(*Note: Jesus would perform seven very poignant miracles on the Shabbat! And this would infuriate the rabbis so much so that they plotted to get rid of Him. How sad!*

He would heal a lame man by the pool of Bethesda, John 5:1–18;
He would drive out an evil spirit Mark, 1:21–28;
He would heal Peter's mother-in-law Mark, 1:29–31;
He would heal a man with a withered hand, Luke 6:6;
He would heal a blind man, John 9:1–16;
A crippled woman would walk again! Luke 13:10–17;
A man with dropsy would live to see another day! Luke 14:1–6)

32
Walking Trees

δενδρα ορω περιπατουντας

🍃

He looked up and said, "I see people;
they look like trees walking around."
Mark 8:24 (NIV)

Jesus enters the sleepy little town of Bethsaida, *"house of fishes."* It was a fishing village that overlooked the blue pristine waters of Lake Tiberius. The city was located in a fertile region where the Jordan River emptied itself in the sea of Galilee. Jesus had performed many miracles in this region. He had fed the 5,000, and it was on these plains that He had time and again slipped away from the noisy crowds and spent the early morning hours with His Father. Next to Jerusalem, this was the most important place where Jesus moved, walked, talked, and lived! *People knew Him there!*

Not too far from Bethsaida lived Philip, Andrew, Peter, James, and John. In fact, tradition says that Peter was born in this sleepy little village and moved later to Capernaum when he got married! There was a gentle warm spring from Bethsaida that ran into the cold waters of the lake, and it was here that fish gathered and spawned. *The fishermen loved this little village and its waters!*

190

The hills around the village were rocky and dotted with olive trees. Small winding narrow roads crisscrossed this hill side. During the springtime the dry hillside exploded with green grass, red poppies, and the flowers of spring. The spring thaw of the winter's snow from Mt. Hermon filled the Jordan River as it emptied at Bethsaida. The sound of gentle streams and the song of bulbuls and thrushes and warblers punctuated the hillside. It seemed that heaven almost touched the earth in this idyllic little village nestled in the hills of Galilee!

The blind man is bewildered! A group of people had seized him from his peaceful home. They had brought him to Jesus. Jesus in turn had dragged him outside the city. He then spits on him. All this is confusing, and the blind man does not speak. Once again the man had requested nothing from anyone, let alone eyes to see!

Bethsaida was on the northern end of the Sea of Galilee. The land was ideal for growing, figs, pomegranates, walnuts, and wild flowers. By March, the slopes of the hills became lusciously green, and the gentle breeze and the early morning mists watered this dry and arid land! Because of the natural beauty of Galilee, the Roman nobility and high-ranking officials settled here. With that came new languages, dialects, and foreigners with strange customs. The Romans used Greek to converse and to do business, and as such, it would have been likely that the Galileans were fluent in Greek and in Aramaic. Aramaic was used in the synagogues to teach and to preach. There was so much international traffic in and around Galilee that even the local Galileans spoke with an accent and could be easily identified as being from Galilee! The Galileans were rough and rugged and had a reputation of being trouble makers! The Galileans were not tolerant of the Romans, and the Romans in turn despised the Galileans. Jesus ben-Yosef was a Galilean!

Being blind was a curse from God. Being blind in Galilee was a double curse! The population was so varied and diverse that one could not understand one's own standing in the community. A high priest could not be a high priest if he had defective eye sight. A blind animal could not be sacrificed. A goat, a sheep, or a heifer that was blind was unclean and could not be used as an offering. Look at what happened in our own history! The people of Sodom and the army of the Syrian king during Elisha's days were blinded by angels. The Torah clearly stated that YHWH causes blindness. Being blind was a serious illness that had its origin from YHWH! Therefore, a blind man was shunned and persecuted and lived a solitary life in silence and in darkness. *I was that man. I was a despised Galilean blind man, but I was not a beggar!*

Mark says that they (we do NOT know who) *brought* him (the BLIND man) to Jesus, and they *begge*d (we do NOT know who) Jesus to heal him. Who are *"THEY"?* Mark does NOT mention that this man was a beggar! He simply says that they *brought* him to Jesus and they *requested* that Jesus heal this man. Both the verbs *"brought"* and *"requested"* are in the present active indicative third person plural. Why is that important? In Greek, the *tense* denotes the *kind* of action! *The subject is performing the action.* In other words, the picture that we get is this: a group of friends *(they)* of the blind man go to his house. *They* get hold of him. *They* grab him. *They* bring him to Jesus. *The action is linear. They* continue to request Jesus for a healing. *They* implore him. *They* beg Him. *They* bother Him. *They* insist that Jesus heal the blind man. *They* keep on until Jesus, responded. While all this time the blind man is quiet! It is all *"they!"* The subject (they) is performing the action. *They* are requesting the healing, not the blind man!

When I read this miracle, the name of Andrew is stamped all over its pages! In my opinion, I believe that a lot of internal evidence points to Andrew being the one that would most likely have brought this blind man to Jesus and would have requested a healing.

Fact: Andrew was from this tiny little village of Bethsaida. Remember, in this village lived Philip, Andrew, Peter, James, and John. It was their home turf! They were aware of all the happenings in this neighborhood. They knew who was sick, who was well, who was rich, who was getting married, who was leaving, who was coming into the village, and who had just died! They were a tightly knit group of Galileans. They were also fishermen, and that meant that they listened to all the gossip in the fish market. It was a small village. I would venture to guess that they all knew who this *blind* man was. He was not a beggar begging in the streets of Bethsaida and crying out to passersby for a morsel of food and some copper coins. He was someone who had friends. Someone who was respected! Someone who was important enough that people were interested in him. Three times Andrew brought people to Jesus: first Simon, his own brother, then the little boy with a lunch of some barley bread and dried fishes, and finally, he brought some of the Gentile Greeks who were looking for Jesus. Could it be that Andrew summoned a number of his friends, and *they* went to the blind man's house and brought him to Jesus? Could it be that this blind man was somehow related to Philip, Andrew, Peter, John, and James who were all from Bethsaida? Could it be that *they* all went to this man's house with Andrew leading the way? Could it be that the *"they"* were actually the disciples? It does make you wonder when you place all the pieces together!

As I read this miracle, another interesting fact jumps out from this incident. Jesus "took" the blind man "outside" the village! Why outside this tiny village? Jesus (Greek: *"epilambomenos"*) *took the man. Literally translated, Jesus seized him, took hold of him, took hold of him, grabbed him, actively taking him, took him by force outside the village. The action of the verb suggests that the subject, Jesus, is performing the action on his own behalf! The subject, Jesus, is intimately involved in the action. Sort of like making clay and placing it on the blind man or like breaking bread in the upper room, or like when He stooped down besides the woman caught in adultery and started writing on the dirt or like when He blessed the children by placing His hands on them. Jesus is actively involved in the healing of this man. The picture that comes to my mind is Jesus dragging this blind man outside the village. The disciples and the group of people who brought him to Jesus are stunned. They asked for a healing, and Jesus is taking this man "outside" the village. It is where this man belonged. Nothing unclean was allowed to live inside the walls of Jerusalem or Bethsaida or any other city. Jesus emphasizes the fact that this is where the man belonged, OUTSIDE, not inside the city! That is how the Creator saw Him. A sinner! But*

Jesus does NOT leave him there! Hallelujah! He accompanies him outside the city. He reminds the man and his friends that this is the rightful place where this man should have been. But this is where Jesus Himself would be. It does not matter where we are, He will be there with us! Outside the city is where the sinners belonged. This is where Jesus would confront us.

The blind man was reminded but grace would stay with him! Grace would shower its blessings upon Him without any prejudice, outside the city! This is where He would heal this blind man! The blind man had no right to be "inside" the city. But grace had all the rights to restore Him outside the city, and grace would bring him "inside" the city completely whole!

The third area of interest is that Jesus "spits" directly into this man's eyes! What a horrible thing to do! They asked for a simple healing. Not all this drama! *They* hoped that Jesus would simply touch this man's eyes and he would receive his eyesight back. *They* had seen Him do that a thousand times. *They* had hoped for a quick resolution to this blindness! At times a mere word from Jesus had healed people, like that centurion's servant who was almost dead! At times Jesus had traveled out of the way to heal a *Syrophoenician Greek* Gentile woman's dead son. At times His look had stopped demons in their tracks. *But not this time.* The disciples could not understand this behavior of Jesus!

The blind man is bewildered! A group of people had seized him from his peaceful home. *They* had brought him to Jesus. Jesus in turn had dragged him outside the city. He then spits on him. All this is confusing, and the blind man does not speak. *Once again the man had requested nothing from anyone,* let alone eyes to see! I am sure that this man felt that he was being abused! He must have felt that everyone, including Jesus, was mocking at His misfortunes. *Yet he is resigned.* Somewhere in the recesses of his mind he is being reminded of the enormity of his sins. He is silent! He is penitent. He is getting his rightful dues. He is worthless! He is a sinner, and there is no hope! *He belongs outside the city and deserved to be spat on, cursed at, laughed at, jeered at, finger-wagged at, and left for dead! His heart cries within him.* He thought he could hide in the shelter of his house for the rest of his days. But he had to come to grips with his past sins. He had to confront his sins.

The demons seemed to agree with Jesus! *"Leave him there!"* they shriek and dance! But once again, grace steps in. Mercy marches on uninvited. Love would restore that which hate had destroyed! *Light would pierce through his darkness, uninvited!*

A voice breaks thru this man's bewildered mind. A voice that interrogates, demands; *a voice that neither asks him to recite all his past sins nor does it question his present unworthiness. It neither forces a confession nor does it offer forgiveness. It simply demands. It orders. It confronts. It breaks through the silence of yesterday and marches into the reality of the present and assures the promise of the future. "Open your eyes and tell me if you see anything!" Who could disobey the Voice of God! He opens his eyes, expecting nothing but darkness. But instead, he sees "men like trees, walking!" Blurred inaccurate vision! Disappointment! What is worse than blindness is partial and dwarfed sight! At least in darkness he could be silent. With blurred elongated and inaccurate vision he would be battered and would have to strain to see through all his inaccuracies! Not a happy feeling!*

This baffles me. Why would Jesus do that? Why would He perform a miracle that would appear to be *"incomplete"*? This is the first and ONLY time that He would perform an "incomplete" miracle! Was someone's obvious lack of faith keeping this man from receiving the full extent of this blessing?

Could it be that, like Elijah's searching the sky seven times for the clouds, this man was repeatedly reminded of his unworthiness? Could it be that this man's sins were of such great intensity and magnitude that he needed to be *"washed" twice?*

Could it be that no one was interceding on a daily basis for this lost son of Abraham?

Could it be that the demons of hell had such a strong hold on him that the Prince of heaven's mighty army had to intervene not once but *twice* on his behalf?

Could it be that this man's repentance was only complete the *second* time?

Could it be that this man needed a *two-fold grace?*

Could it be that there are sins so intense in our own lives that even the Son of God has to touch us not once but twice to completely restore us from the eclipse of our deep and powerful sins?

I can only speculate!

The second time, Jesus laid His hands on his eyes! This time the man's eyesight was totally restored.

First his hands drag him outside the city; next He spits on the blind man. Then He speaks to him providing *partial eyesight*. Finally He lays His hands on his eyes for *complete restoration*. All that done without a single request from the blind man! Astonishing!

He sees! He rejoices! His sins are forgiven! His eyesight is restored!

Let me leave you with a final thought!

The sky is black. Clouds of impending storm brood overhead! A fleshless skeleton slumbers in a long-forgotten tomb. Cobras slither through the windows of its hollow sockets. Darkness bred with my own accusing conscience choke my lonely and forgotten soul. The skeleton howls within me.

Are You there? Can You see me?

I can't breathe!

The Voice of God breaks through!

Not once, but twice! He drags me into His light!

Light engulfs the tomb! Cobras retreat into darkness as the skeleton comes to life! From darkness to light to life and beyond...

33

Dropsy

υδρωπικος

Jesus asked the Pharisees and experts in the law, "Is it lawful to
heal on the Sabbath or not?" But they remained silent. So taking
hold of the man, he healed him and sent him on his way.
Luke 14:3 (NIV)

The Setting: It was a trap and Jesus walked right into it!
Look! There were Pharisees and lawyers of the law under the
roof of the *Ruler* of the Pharisees! There was *Jesus*, the troublemaker
who was the invited guest; a Lamb among ravenous wolves! Then
there was the sick, distorted, and distended man who was obviously
bloated and edematous due to *hudropikos,* a disease that was the
result of a multi-systems failure! Obviously his liver, kidneys,
circulatory system, heart, and limbs were all malfunctioning. What
was this sinner who was cursed by *Elohim,* doing in the house of
the *Ruler* of the Pharisees, who was blessed by *Elohim* and who had
specific rules against socializing with the likes of this sinner?

Luke, who was a physician, uses some very interesting and poignant verbs to denote the actions of the setting in which the miracle
is couched. He states that the lawyers were *"scrutinizing" (Greek:
parateiromenoi)* Jesus. He states that the sick man was placed

197

He saw them all. The conniving lawyers, the distended sick man, the staged witnesses, the anxious disciples, the unseen holy angels, and the accuser of the brethren in the shadows! How His heart ached for each one of them! He loved every one of them!

"directly" (*Greek: emprosthen*) in front of Jesus. Shouldn't this man have been placed *outside* the house of the Ruler of the Pharisees if the purpose of the sick man to visit the house of the Ruler of the Pharisees was to procure some scraps from the Sabbath dinner? Shouldn't he have been placed in the shadows of the servant quarters? No! He is placed in the direct line of fire. It is almost pathetic. *Sinful man tries to entrap God!* Heaven must have shaken its head with disbelief! Angels must have whispered in hushed voices. And we as spectators in the era of iPads and Starbucks and Retina computers slowly begin to unfold this fantastic story of the entrapment of Son of God by a group of lawyers stuck away in the house of a Ruler of the Pharisees on a Sabbath day when God never rests!

The Bait. The Sick Man: I can barely walk. My stomach is distended. My hands are swollen. My legs are huge and filled with water. I have pitting edema all over the body! I gasp as I struggle to get from one place to another. I am always short of breath! My heart most of the times seems like it is going to explode. I had abused my life as a young man, and now my liver and kidneys were hopelessly sick. My body could not expel all the liquids. I was a sick man. I am sure you have seen people like me walking the streets. This is what can happen when you live a life that is abusive. The physicians in my village called it *"water disease!"* I called it *walking death, congestive heart failure!*

It was just a matter of time before my wasting and weak heart would refuse to pump any more, my lungs would fill with my own fluids, and I would drown and slip into the sleep of death. What was this life that I was living? Barely existing and getting along. I was a deformed, distorted specter of sickness. Children were scared of me, and the people who were once my friends avoided me. It was a struggle even to get up from my bed. It was a struggle to put my clothes on, to go to the bathroom, to walk around; everything was a struggle. My body was bent, tired, and contorted! I do not blame anyone for this disease. I was resigned to the inevitable visit by the grim reaper. Just a matter of time, then it will all be over. *Can't wait for that to happen!*

I had no quality of life! When was the last time I had been to a wedding or a funeral, or a synagogue or a marketplace, or, for that matter, when was it that anyone had invited me to their house? I was just a nobody drowning in self-pity and caught in a web of feelings that are so hard to describe! This world was only for those who were able to survive in it, like I once had when I was living that raucous life! I lived in the past excitement and hated the present reality. *What am I?* A soul trapped in a distorted body that was drowning in its own fluids. One day, my body would drown! That was the reality, and no one could stop this! I wish someone, anyone would be kind to me! I wonder if God would hear me. Then I got an invitation for a Shabbat meal to the house of the Ruler of the Pharisees! I could barely believe my ears!

The Hunter. The Ruler of the Pharisees: "Sh'ma Yis'rael Adonai Eloheinu Adonai echad. . ." (Hear O Israel, YHWH is our God and YHWH is one. . .) Ah! The words of the *Shema* have such sweetness extolling the virtues of the One True God! How dare this *ben-Yosef* claim equality with the One True God! We need to put Him to test! This has gone far enough. Who does He think He is, walking through our cities and villages and healing people on the Holy Sabbath day and claiming to have God as *His Father*? Such blasphemy! Such arrogance! How can this man whose lineage is doubtful and whose parentage is questionable claim to be the *"Christos"*? Just because He has a group of followers does not make Him the *"Mashiach." We, the Pharisees, had not evaluated Him, and we had not placed our stamp of approval on this renegade Rabbi from Nazareth! We had been "set apart" to protect the Torah! There were too many of these characters running around our villages destroying the Law. We need to trap this ben-Yosef! We need to bring back the teachings of the Torah to the forefront. We need to eliminate this problem before it is too late. Nothing else matters at this point! We need proof, and*

Heaven's Short List!

we need witnesses! This Jesus must be dealt with immediately and surgically without prejudice and dispatched to a Roman cross!

The best way would be to invite him to my house along with the lawyers, those that knew the *Torah,* the *Laws of Moses,* and entrap him! We will provide him with a situation, and He will not be able to back Himself out of it! We will watch Him like a hawk! We will document every move that He makes, and we will have witnesses and lawyers and scribes. We will make Him dig His own grave! I will invite Him to my house on the *Shabbat,* along with my trusted cohorts, and then I will bring in the most despicable and distorted sick man that I can find in the village and place him right in the path of *ben-Yosef,* and if He heals this man on the *Qodesh ha yom Shabbat (the Holy Sabbath Day),* we have a case for prosecution and eventual punishment! We will play on His emotions!

In fact I know just the right person to invite. That distorted excuse of a human being who had the *"water disease". . .God!* I am so glad I am not like that man cursed by Elohim. *May God be praised!* I wonder if my house would become unclean if I allowed this creature of sin to wander into my premises! All that matters now is that we trap Jesus. Well, after the fact I can perform a cleansing ritual and offer a dove or a lamb as a sin offering, and that would cleanse me from impurity! If He heals him, He would be breaking the Shabbat, and if He cannot heal him, we will call this Rabbi a phony! It is a no-win situation for *ben-Yosef!* Really, when was the last time anyone has heard a man being cured instantaneously of the dreaded "*water* disease?" This should be fun! Yes! That is exactly what I will do! What a brilliant idea! *And we will do this on the Shabbat!*

(Could it be that such grievous and heinous thoughts might have invaded the mind of a Ruler of the Pharisees as he evaluated the problem that was in front of him? Ben-Yosef the Rabbi from Nazareth had become a thorn in their side. He had to be eliminated!)

The Hunted. GOD! It was the Sabbath day. A day when God rested from all His works, or *did He?* God went to the synagogue. It was His custom, and that is where He would be. Wonder if He knew He was walking into a trap set by the Ruler of the Pharisees! *Of course He did! He was God in three dimensions doing what He*

200

does best! Restoration, redemption and reinstatement! Patching up distorted humanity!

He was invited after the Sabbath service to the house of the Ruler of the Pharisees! That in itself was a big honor. You watched yourself and made sure that you were irreproachable when it came to matters of the Law. The Hunter was an *"archonton,"* a ruler. The ruler had invited God to his house! Not everyone was invited to be in the presence of the Ruler of the Pharisees. They made the Law! They upheld the Law. They protected the Law. They were the experts of the Law! *They were the Law!* This group of people were high up on the ecclesiastical ladder. This was an elite club consisting of people of wealth, importance, and influence.

A sumptuous Shabbat meal was set before the guests. Guarded opulence would have been the word of the day. The guests' feet would have been washed by a slave. Designated seats would have been marked for the prominent invitees. The most important guests would have been given the reclining seat beside the Ruler of the Pharisees. The *Kiddush* and the *Hamotzie* blessings would have been said. The meal would have been served: fish, lamb, soup, and bread made from barley or rye or wheat, and goat cheese, olives, dates, and pomegranates would have graced the menu. The meal would have been sumptuous being that it was in the house of the Ruler of the Pharisees. No small detail would have been left unattended!

After the meal there would be the customary discussion regarding the fine matters of the Law, which would have lulled even the mightiest orator to sleep! There would be discussions and parsing of terms and expounding the *Torah* according to various schools of the Pharisees. But the basic tenet could not be violated. The *Torah* will be respected, and there would be no deviations from the basic tenets of the law, the writings of *Moshe,* God's servant!

This was the moment that the disciples were waiting for. One word of support from the Ruler of the Pharisees and that would be enough! This was an important meeting. If Jesus and the twelve disciples could have the open support of the *Ruler* of the Pharisees, that would be priceless! This would be a great opportunity for Jesus to set things right; to iron out differences. They could accomplish so much without the constant obstacles and the accusations that they faced from the religious leaders each day

God restores! God heals! God rescues! God overcomes! God sets free! God loves!

God was being hunted for the worse by a band of renegade priests! The stage was set.

His divine heart must have been torn into a thousand pieces as He saw the story unfolding in front of Him. He saw them all as Humanity, with a capital *"H,"* lost in sin and caught in a web of confusion. They were not the ones to blame. *It was the Accuser.* He had clouded their minds with such confusion that no one, not even the keepers of the Law and the rulers of the synagogue were immune from the attacks of that mighty angel who was once the covering cherub in the Most Holy Place. How tragic! Truth was trampled on the rocks of hopelessness. *Everything was a mess.* The works of Lucifer need to be unraveled, painfully. In time, Lucifer will be exposed on earth and in heaven! The damage that was done by that covering cherub would have to be restored by none other than the Creator who had created this angel of light!

He saw them all. The conniving lawyers, the distended sick man, the staged witnesses, the anxious disciples, the unseen holy angels, and the accuser of the brethren in the shadows! How His heart ached for each one of them! He loved every one of them! He would have to restore all of them, and that would cost Him. That would lead Him to a Roman cross outside the walls of the Holy City! But they were worth it all!

He unravels each of the lives, knowing very well that He could be and would be mistaken, misunderstood, and, finally, crucified. He forges on any way. Stubborn Love would risk it all and would take the bait!

Question: Is it lawful to heal on the Shabbat?
Response: Silence

Jesus brings the sick man and heals him!

Question: If your son or your ox fell into a well on the Shabbat, would you pull them out immediately or leave him there?
Response: Silence

Sandwiched between two questions is the miracle.

The sick man is healed on the Shabbat. Witnesses have seen the blatant violation of the Shabbat regulation. The lawyers and the scholars have taken ample notes. The stage is set for the prosecution of Jesus, *ben-Yosef*, the Son of God! There are no thankful words spoken by the sick man or a "thank you" from the ruler of the synagogue. Nothing! Heaven witnesses in disbelief as demons of hell plot in the shadows.

He came to His own, and His own rejected Him! He loved us, and we hated Him! He fed us, and we refused Him a drink of water as He was dying! He healed us, and we crucified Him! All because He was trying to restore us, heal us, and revive us. But as many as received Him, He gave them power to be called the Sons of God and made us heirs to the throne of God! He was the *"Miracle"* in every story! He is the Miracle in my story. *That day in a house of the Ruler of the Pharisees, heaven watched with disbelief as earth and hell plotted to entrap God on the Holy Sabbath Day!*

(*Note: Jesus would perform seven very poignant miracles on the Shabbat! And this would infuriate the rabbis so much so that they plotted to get rid of Him. How sad!*

He would heal a lame man by the pool of Bethesda, John 5:1–18;
He would drive out an evil spirit Mark, 1:21–28;
He would heal Peter's mother-in-law Mark, 1:29–31;
He would heal a man with a withered hand, Luke 6:6;
He would heal a blind man, John 9:1–16;
A crippled woman would walk again! Luke 13:10–17;
A man with dropsy would live to see another day! Luke 14:1–6)

34
Malchus' Ear

το ους το δεξιον

And one of them struck the servant of the high priest, cutting off his right ear. But Jesus answered, "No more of this!" And he touched the man's ear and healed him.
Luke 22:50–51 (NIV)

I am *Malchus,* the personal servant of *Caiaphas* the High Priest of the Most High God. The venerable Caiaphas was the only one who could enter the Most Holy Place to mediate between God and man. He was sinless, perfect, and holy! He was the only one who could be in the presence of YHWH once a year and live to tell about it! He was a direct descendent of Aaron, the brother of Moses!

It was I who made sure that the high priest's blue robe with golden bells and pomegranates on its hems were secured without any blemish. It was I who made sure that the precious *ephod* with the names of the twelve tribes and the breastplate with the twelve precious stones with the *Urim* and the *Thummim* and the linen turban with its golden inscription *"Holiness to YHWH"* secured with a blue ribbon, were all perfect and without any fault. Nothing unholy would survive the Presence in the Most Holy Place on the Day of Atonement, the tenth day of the seventh month when my master entered the Most Holy Place in the temple! Every stitch, every bell, every pomegranate had to be secured without a flaw! On this day of Atonement Caiaphas sprinkled the blood on the mercy seat and asked for forgiveness of all the people of Israel. This was a solemn day and a holy duty. Once you were a high priest, you remained a high priest as long as you lived. And if you were his servant, you remained with him as long as you lived.

Then I saw Him bending down in the dirt, kneeling in front of me, searching for my ear in the dirt in the flames of the flickering Roman torches... He picked it up and came close to me and attached it to my face! I was speechless!

But today was not Yom Kipper, the Day of Atonement; it was the Passover weekend! We had so much to do. It was the day when Israel was delivered from the land of *Mizraim (Egypt)*. It was the day when the angel of death marched through *Mizraim* and struck down the firstborn whose house was not marked with the blood of a spotless and perfect lamb! It was the only day you ate and slept fully clothed and with shoes on your feet! The garments had to be made ready. The shoes had to be polished. The utensils had to be set in order.

The lambs had to be checked and rechecked to make sure that they were without any blemish. The *korban Pesach* (the Passover lamb) had to be made ready for the family. The lamb had to be one year old, perfect and faultless. No hidden blemishes would be tolerated! It was the lamb for the high priest's family. The unleavened *matzo* bread, the meat, the bitter herbs, the wine, the cups—*everything* had to be perfect. Even the pomegranate wood for the roasting of the lamb had to be heated just right. It could not send out too much smoke or burn out before the meat is cooked!

My master came from a great family of high priests. His father-in- law, *Annas*, was a high priest, and he made sure that all of his five sons *Eleazer, Jonathan, Theophilus, Matthias, and Ananus* all became high priests. He also made sure that my master

Joseph-ben-Caiaphas, who was married to his daughter, became a high priest. Thus, my master Caiaphas was married into a family of high priests! He was feared and well respected by the Romans as well as the local Jews. I was constantly in the presence of holiness. He was the supreme religious leader of the Israelites. What he said was the religious law of Israel! He was perfect and blameless. I, who was his personal servant, could not afford to have any blemish! While I was in the service of *Caiaphas, Annas,* his father-in-law, was also the high priest! I was the ears and the mouth of the venerable Caiaphas, the priest of YHWH. Since my master could not officially leave the temple courts, I became his representative on multiple occasions. He, along with *Annas,* his father-in-law, controlled the temple activities. Nothing escaped their watchful eyes. I was the ears and eyes of the entire high priest family!

All this changed when *ben-Yosef* entered the Temple and claimed to be God!

Who wants to be out in the middle of the night with some unclean Roman Gentiles chasing down a rebel who was hiding in some olive groves beyond the walls of this holy city, I mumbled to myself as I led this group of assassins. I did not want to do this! I had so much to do! Besides, we could have easily arrested this man, who I was supposed to bring to my master's presence, in the temple. He had frequented the temple grounds quite a few times! Sometimes the plans and requests of the high priest made no sense! But you did not question Caiaphas. That meant instant death. Besides, I was only his servant. I do what my master tells me!

This was the plan: Jesus ben-Yosef needed to be arrested. He had claimed to be God's Son, and he had also claimed to be the King of the Jews! As such, he was in violation of both the laws of the temple and the laws of Augustus Caesar. He would be punished according to Jewish and Roman laws. That only meant death by crucifixion! I would lead the arrest. I would represent Caiaphas! My master had called me earlier today when one of the followers of this man Jesus had volunteered to betray him for a few pieces of silver. This man, *Judas ben-Iscariot* would lead the procession to the secret place where Jesus was hiding with his band of zealots. By his kiss, Judas would show us who this man Jesus was. He would kiss Jesus on his cheeks, and we would arrest him and bring him to my master's house for questioning. Period!

This was a dangerous mission. Jesus was a rebel who was surrounded by a group of zealots who were going to overthrow the Romans. There would be a fight, and who knows, someone might get hurt or killed. We needed the Romans to protect us. King Herod, who lived very close to my master's house, had given us permission to take a contingency of seasoned Roman guards to accompany the temple guards. We needed all the help, and my master wanted to catch this man Jesus. It was my responsibility to represent the venerable high priest in this arrest. I was in charge of this group, and I would report directly to Caiaphas everything that happened that night. Nothing was left to chance. The plan would be flawless and carried with surgical precision. It was simple but risky. If the man escaped, it would be my responsibility. If the plan was successful, I would be looked upon with great favor by the high priest and King Herod as the man who captured a zealot who had defied Rome and had challenged Jerusalem and I would be rewarded handsomely!

In secrecy we gathered at my master's house. I handpicked the trusted temple guards. Swords were sharpened, and torches were lit. Shoes were tied, and shields were procured! In silence we left my master's house. We stopped at King Herod's palace as a group of Roman royal guards joined our silent and stealthy procession! What a mixture that was. *The clean temple guards in their long white linen and turban and well-kept beards contrasted with the dirty, ruthless Roman soldiers in their short crimson tunics, unshaved faces, bleary red drunken eyes, knee high leather sandals laced to their calves, shiny helmets, and short swords strapped to their waist.* Torches lit up this strange procession, two groups of guards who hated each other but were now joined together with one purpose, to seek and to capture a rebel named Jesus who was hiding in the hills outside the walls of Jerusalem in an obscure garden!

We snaked our way past Herod's palace, past the Sanhedrin and the walls of the glistening temple, through the sleeping suburbs where the aristocracy lived, out the city through the *sheep gate,* and descended into the Kidron Valley, which would soon be filled with the blood of a thousand sacrificial lambs from the Passover. I gathered my robe and held it to my knee as we crossed the muddy Kidron Valley. We then followed the road to Bethany and climbed a small hill. Right at the junction where the road took a fork, one leading north to Jericho and the other south east to Bethany was the place where Judas summoned us to a halt. We stopped. He pointed us to the Garden. *The Garden of Gethsemane.* He whispered that it was here, among the olive trees, that Jesus was hiding with his followers. He warned us to be cautious and reminded that this man possessed strange and curious powers! I was right besides Judas as he led us. The Romans soldiers were ahead of us!

Swords drawn, the Roman royal guard led the group cautiously, often stopping to assess the situation. Behind them came the temple guards. The flames from the torches cast strange and unholy shadows in the olive grove. The pungent smell of sweat mixed with smoke from the torches cut through the clean olive grove like a double-ended Philistine dagger! The eerie sound of our muffled footsteps punctuated the chirp of the hillside crickets. *The yellow eyes of a silent owl in the tree danced in the flames as a hungry wolf howled in the hills surrounding the garden.* It almost seemed like another army was following us! Fear and anticipation slowly wrapped their claws around my throat! The dust and the smell of smoke and the anticipation of the unexpected suffocated my fearful heart! I was not used to this! What if this group of zealots put up a fight? What if the entire city of Bethany and the unclean mob that frequented these hills decided to come against us? This Jesus had quite a following*! What if he was waiting for us!* Every flickering shadow cast by the torches seemed to be hiding a zealot! I clutched my sword a little tighter. My job was in the safety of my master's house. I had never gone on a nighttime raid before. I am not a fighter even though tonight I carried a sword in my hand. I was covered with dirt and dust and sweat! I wanted to leave! I need to worry about the Passover meal! *Too late!*

Judas pointed to something! We moved closer! I could see the frame of a group of people illuminated by the dancing flames of the torches. The Roman guard shouted, *"Halt!"*

Judas ran ahead of us and kissed the cheeks of a scrubby man in his early thirties. That was the cue! The Roman guards rushed to grab him. Then all pandemonium broke loose. There were shouts and flashing blades. A sword fight had commenced. I tried to run away, and then *I felt the cold blade from a sword glance the right side of my head.* I felt a sharp pain. I could feel warm blood oozing from my ear, soaking my white temple clothes. I must be dying, I thought. The pain was excruciating, but my fear of dying was stronger. It dawned on me that without the ear, I would be imperfect and would not be able to serve in the family of Caiaphas, the High Priest! *My future was decimated. I would be "unclean!" I would be sent away and dismissed for an act that I did not commit!* Why me? Why now? A voice, no a command, split the dark night! *"Peter, put away that sword!" Then I saw Him bending down in the dirt, kneeling in front of me, searching for my ear in the dirt in the flames of the flickering Roman torches.* He picked it up and came close to me and attached it to my face! I was speechless! Who is this man that I had come to arrest? Who is this man that can attach a knifed ear back to the body? My being whole was more important to Him than His own life! Who was this man that would remember me in the midst of His own arrest? I was terrified! I could not stand in front of this man! I fled from the garden. I ran all the way back to Caiaphas's house, stumbling in the dark as an unknown power possessed me. I wanted nothing to do with this man. I wanted nothing to do with this arrest! I had to prepare for the Passover meal. . .or *was it too late?*

They arrested him that night and brought Him before Caiaphas. I didn't even know the man! By the time the Romans were finished with Him, He was bruised and bleeding and beaten, just a shell of a man. From the shadows I watched Him through those *five trials. He was shuffled from Annas, to Caiaphas, to the Sanhedrin, to Pilate and to Herod, and then back to Pilate! He was executed by the Romans. They said that even death could not hold Him in the grave!*

The picture that is etched in my mind is that of this Man kneeling in front of me, a servant, a slave, surrounded by Roman soldiers, and dying torches, searching the dirt in the Garden of Gethsemane for my ear, the day He was arrested and condemned to die! What kind of a man was He? We had come to arrest Him and to execute Him, but here He was searching for my ear! I was the only one that got hurt that day! Had He not healed me, I would have been unclean. . .I was the only one that was healed that day. . .I would never be the same. . .I would remember Him every Passover! I would remember Him every time I touched my right ear!

Was He God?

Wish I had all the answers!

I must get ready for the Passover meal. . .I had so much to do!

The End!

References

Sick –Disease (12)
(1) One Leper Matt 8
(24) Ten Lepers Lk 17:11-18
(23) Bethesda Jn 5:1-9
(6) Paralytic Mt 9
(8) Sick Woman 12 yrs Lk 8:43
(11) Withered hand Lk 6:6
(15) Syro Phoenician
Woman Mk 7:24
(2) Centurions Servant Mt 8
(3) Peters Mother in law Mt 8
(31) Crippled woman 18 years
Lk 13:10-17
(26) Noble man's son Jn 4:46-54
(33) Malchus' ear Lk 22:50

Death (3)
(7) Jairus' Daughter Lk 8
(25) Nain Lk 7:11-17
(29) Lazarus Jn 11:38-44

Mute + Demon (6)
(17) Mute son Matt 17:14-20, Mark
9:14-29, Lk 9:37-43, Mk 9:17
(22) Deaf Mute Mk7:31
(10) Mute Demoniac Mt 9:33
(12) Mute, Blind Demoniac Mt 12:22
(5) Demoniacs Mt 8
(21) Lonely Demoniac Mk 1

Food (4)
(13) 5000+ Jn 6:1-14
(16) 4000+ Mt 15: 29-38
(27) Cana Jn 2:1-11
(28) Fish Jn 21:1-14

Blind (4)
(9) 2 Blind men Mt 9:27
(19) Bartimaeus Mk 10:46
(30) Man born blind Jn 9:1-41
(32) Bethsaida blind man Mk 8:22-26

Sabbath Miracles (7)
(23) Bethesda John 5:1-18;
(21) Lonely Demoniac
Mark 1:21-28;
(3) Peter's mother-in-law
Mark 1:29-31;
(11) Withered hand Lk 6:6
(30) Man born blind John 9:1-16;
(31) Crippled woman Luke 13:10-
17; (34) A man with dropsy would
live to see another day! Luke 14:1-6

Nature (2)
(4) Storm Mt 8
(14) Storm Mt 14: 22-30

Strange (2)
(18) Fish and the Drachma
Mt 17:24-27
(20) Fig Tree Mk 11:13

About the Author

S am Thomas was born in India and grew up in Ethiopia. He holds a BA in Theology and a BA in Biblical languages from Walla Walla University. He has a Masters in Divinity from Andrews University Theological Seminary with an emphasis in Near Eastern Languages. He has a certificate of chaplaincy. He holds a Doctorate in Dental Surgery from Loma Linda University and a PhD in Biblical Studies. He is an ordained Minister of the Gospel and a Biblical Scholar. He is fluent in multiple languages. He has traveled extensively in the Middle East, Africa, and around the world.

His passions are World Missions, providing medical and dental relief to those around the world and proclaiming the imminent return of our Lord and Savior Jesus Christ, the Son of God!

It is when we are alone and surrounded by silence that we hear the Voice of God beckoning us for an intimate and a closer communion with Him. He speaks in the silence of our hearts and communes with us in the stillness of our souls and thunders when darkness consumes our frail and bleeding hearts!

CPSIA information can be obtained
at www.ICGtesting.com
Printed in the USA
FSOW03n2032290118
43960FS